A WISCONSIN

COUNTY PARKS

OF WISCONSIN

600 PARKS YOU CAN VISIT
FEATURING 25 FAVORITES

■

JEANNETTE & CHET BELL

WISCONSIN TRAILS
Madison, Wisconsin

Library of Congress Catalog Card Number: 96-061192
ISBN: 0-915024-54-3

Editor: Elizabeth McBride
Editorial interns: Heather Harlan, Sally Sosnouski
Designer: Jane Tenenbaum
Cover design: Kathie Campbell
Production: KC Graphics
Cover photograph: Darryl Beers, Goodman Park, Marinette County

Printed in the United States of America by Master Litho.

The publisher gratefully acknowledges county parks offices for their generous assistance and for the use of photographs. Photo credits: Michael Shedlock, pp. 1, 35; Zane Williams, p. 17; Darryl Beers, p. 24.

WISCONSIN TRAILS
P.O. Box 5650
Madison, WI 53705
(800) 236-8088

To our children,
Chester, Colleen and Edith,
who as youth enhanced the enjoyment of our family camping trips.

Wisconsin Counties

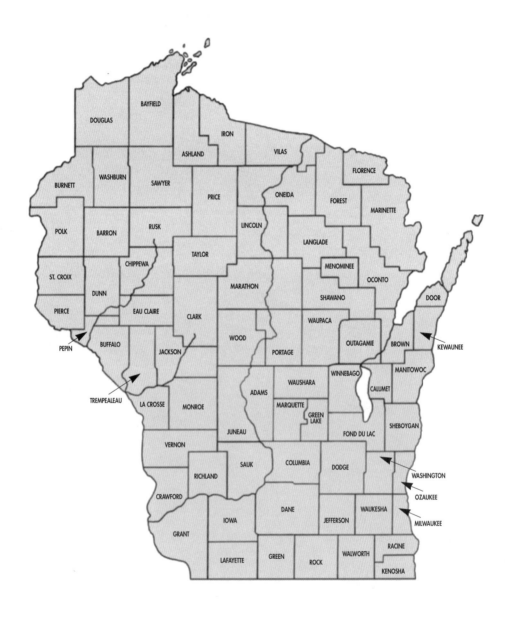

Contents

25 Favorite County Parks   1

Best Parks for Special Uses   35

Guide to County Parks   55

Introduction

Our project, visiting Wisconsin's county parks, began in 1991. Chet and I had always enjoyed touring the state's back roads. In fact, one of our greatest pleasures was to take a book of county maps and route our trips using alternatives to major highways. This was a slower method of travel, of course, but it provided us with a beautiful and sometimes awesome view of our wonderful state. In our travels, we always noted the existence of county parks, which were often welcome rest stops on long journeys. Somewhere along the way we decided to visit as many as we could and collect information about them. It was a grand experience, and one that we are sorry to see end.

Over five years, we visited hundreds of county parks. Every time we traveled in Wisconsin, we included stops. A convention in Superior, for example, enabled us to see parks on the way up, and a slow route home allowed for a continuation of the task. Long weekends and, at times, entire vacations were dedicated to this endeavor. Working steadily, we were able to visit as many as 10 or 12 parks in a single day. Of course, that meant all we could enjoy in each was a picnic lunch or a quick hike. But frequently we were able to return another time and stay longer.

We found county parks to be extremely varied. Most provide facilities for traditional activities like picnicking, camping, boating, hiking and softball. But many are unique in their offerings. We visited parks where you can go caving or venture on a horseback-camping trip or camp along an ATV trail. Some parks preserve one-of-a-kind folk art sites or distinctive geology. While numerous parks feature active recreation (hiking, downhill skiing or even winter innertubing), others revolve around more passive pursuits—looking at wildflowers, viewing a beautiful valley, sitting by a waterfall.

We developed a system for data collection, always recording park facilities and distinguishing characteristics. While most parks were in fine condition, we noted any maintenance problems we saw. If a park was not up to par, we called later to see if improvements had been made. And we acquired a few favorites— parks that especially appealed to us because they enable visitors to do something really special, because they have an outstanding facility, or simply because they are extremely beautiful. All of that information is gathered for you here.

Readers should be aware that finding a county park can sometimes be difficult. The official state highway map suggests the location of many county parks, but it is not always up to date or accurate. Some counties post signs directing you to parks, but most do not. That means guessing and driving until the park is found. For us, this was sometimes an exciting challenge but other times a chore, especially when the park proved to be not particularly notable. In a very few cases, we gave up looking because we couldn't find anything resembling a park. In these situations, we obtained information by contacting the appropriate person in the county government. We include here what we hope are precise directions. Still, it's a good idea to carry in your car either county maps or the *Wisconsin Atlas & Gazetteer*, published by the DeLorme Mapping Co. and available in bookstores.

A note on fees: Some county parks charge admission for day use. We note those that do, but do not give amounts since they likely will change over time. Many parks charge a fee to use a boat landing, and, with very little exception, fees are charged for camping. Since these fees are used to help pay for upkeep, we think you'll agree that they are nominal given the extraordinary service county parks provide.

Jeannette Bell

Country byways meander beside rivers, next to lakes, over hills and into valleys, leading travelers to quaint towns and old farmsteads. Traveling them is a refreshing change from cruising busy and boring freeways. For our county parks travels, Jeannette was the chief navigator, plotting numerous routes. With a briefcase beside her ankles, maps and notepads covering her lap, she was intensely possessed about visiting as many parks as possible, becoming exuberant as we neared the entrance of each destination. We covered thousands of miles. They were fun miles, beautiful miles, stormy miles and memorable miles.

This project exceeded our expectations in terms of enjoyment, while satisfying our appetite for curiosity; ultimately, it resulted in a collection of experiences we wanted to share. It was thrilling to see a doe with her fawn, watch a large turtle crossing the roadway, discover an eagle perched on a broken utility pole, or spot a fox leaving a yard with its prey in its mouth. Sunsets were spectacular. In winter, frost on shrubs and tree branches sparkled like delicate crystal.

As a result of our travels, we gained a great appreciation for Wisconsin's natural resources and the care that they receive. Only in one instance were we disappointed to learn that vandals so frequently trashed a beautiful, remote park site that local maintenance crews saw its restoration as a futile effort. We could sense their disgust with people who ruin facilities intended for community enjoyment. We found the majority of parks, however, whether "pocket" parks, boat landings or large, multiple-use areas, to be well-maintained, and we commend those who administer to them with such obvious vigilance and pride.

If you go on your own county parks adventure, let me suggest that you forget the clock and let the sun be your timepiece! Get in the car and go. Rid yourself of time schedules. Instead of a traditional noon meal, enjoy an impromptu picnic in a park or an early-afternoon lunch in a small-town coffeeshop, savoring homemade pie along with your surroundings. Look forward to getting lost! It's an opportunity to see more of the countryside and, perhaps, more wildlife. Eventually, you'll get back on course and complete the day's journey. Take turns driving. A fresh set of eyes scanning the scenery might observe things the other person would miss. And if you and your partner have been spending too much time apart, you'll find county parks adventuring an excellent way to be together. Because Jeannette and I shared all the components—planning, packing, traveling, getting lost, shopping, eating, sleeping, hiking—we added an element of romance to our travels, and the experience was greatly enriched.

We have done the best we could to verify the information presented here, but if you should find errors or omissions, please write us, care of County Parks, Wisconsin Trails, P.O. Box 5650, Madison, WI 53705. We hope you enjoy your explorations of Wisconsin's great county parks!

Chet Bell

25 Favorite County Parks

Ledge View Nature Center

Calumet County

The first thing you notice when you enter Ledge View Nature Center is a large, magnificent field of colorful wildflowers with a cloud of butterflies hovering over it. But this is only one of the features that makes this county park special. In addition to the restored prairie, the 105-acre park contains fascinating caves. Naturalists offer special programs and guided hikes to help visitors understand and appreciate this unique area.

The ledge upon which Ledge View sits is known as the Niagara Escarpment, a limestone formation that begins in New York State, runs west to Niagara Falls, then disappears under Lake Erie before rising again in Door County and running south through Wisconsin, Illinois and Iowa. Within Ledge View, three miles of hiking trails wind along the ledge to scenic overlooks.

View wildlife and explore underground caves at Ledge View Nature Center.

Three caves—Montgomery Cave, Mother's Cave and Carolyn's Caverns—tunnel underground. These can be explored with a naturalist, but be aware that cave exploration can be challenging! Cavers must wear long pants and long-sleeved shirts to protect their limbs, and will get covered with dirt and mud. Here at Ledge View, one underground journey begins with a seven-foot drop and a crawl through a 150-foot-long "squeeze."

Schedules of caving trips and other programs, such as wildflower seed collecting, are posted in the nature center building, which also houses exhibits on plants and animals found in the area. There is a nominal fee for tours and programs. But aside from all the activities, you'll find Ledge View is a lovely spot just for picnicking. We have come here several times, bringing friends with whom we wanted to share this wonderful place.

Ledge View Nature Center is located on Short Road, off County G south of Chilton.

Observation platforms at Husher Park overlook the lovely Kickapoo River Valley.

Husher Park

Crawford County

We vividly remember our visit to this unusual site, even though five years have passed since we were there. It was an overcast, gloomy day in early spring, and we had been driving up and down country roads searching for the place. Finally we found it—only two acres in size and not very clearly marked. The land, at the crest of a hill, seemed to blend into the surrounding farmland. There was a garbage can and two strange-looking platforms facing in different directions, with steps leading to the tops.

We climbed up, of course, to see why they were there. A powerful wind robbed us of breath, but so also did the spectacular view of the Kickapoo River Valley. With no leaves yet on the trees, we could see for miles. Large springs, set against the greyness of the day, sparkled like jewels.

An area historian, Virgil Butteris of Prairie du Chien, later told us that the springs, called Grant Springs, feed the Kickapoo River and provided fresh water to early settlers. The land that is now the park was purchased by the county in 1969 solely to preserve a view of the springs and the river valley. The park (which is more like a wayside) is set at the top of Pohlmann Hill, also known as Husher Ridge. The ridge is probably named for Michael Husher, who farmed the land in the late 1800s.

Though tiny, and with no facilities other than the observation platforms, Husher Park illustrates a goal common to many of the county parks we visited—to protect something that is noteworthy and make it available for public enjoyment. Here, a community (which does not even have a county parks department—Husher Park is maintained by the highway crew) has declared a beautiful panorama worth preserving for future generations.

Husher Park is located on Highway 131 north of Wauzeka.

Stewart Park

Dane County

Mt. Horeb is the "Troll Capital of the World," and woodcarvings of these little beings greet visitors traveling along Main Street. But in a charming park just outside town, you can almost visualize real-life trolls climbing on the rocks and peeking around trees.

Stewart Park is a lovely spot. Located in the unglaciated area of Wisconsin, it is sited on two levels connected by a winding road. Manmade, spring-fed Stewart Lake, which was created by damming a tributary of Blue Mounds Creek, is the center of attention on the lower level. Around it are rocky banks topped by lush, green trees. Anglers, hoping to catch trout and bass, fish from shore or

Spring-fed Stewart Lake draws anglers, picnickers and hikers to Stewart Park.

from canoes, which can be launched from a designated landing. Picnic tables, a shelter and playground are available for day use. Hiking paths meander past the lake and up the cliff to the upper reaches of the park. In winter, the steep paths are groomed to make scenic and challenging cross-country ski trails.

Stewart Park was established in 1912. Local residents Gabe Mickelson, Andrew Hoff and Sidney Sylvester founded the Lake Park Association, and by October of that year solicited contributions of $100 each from 54 men. With the funds, they purchased the land, built a road, and constructed the dam that formed the lake. The dam was completed on Saturday, Dec. 6, and by the following Monday enough water had filled the lake to allow a group of men to row across.

Lake Park, as it was originally called, was a popular spot for winter sports. Newspaper accounts from 1913 reported 50 spectators on New Year's Day after the lake froze over and, later in the winter, 165 people out ice-skating. In 1914, a ski "slide" was built, and skiers came from as far away as Norway to compete in a ski-jumping tournament. The following year, the tournament attracted 5,000 spectators.

Ice from the lake was harvested and sold to nearby creameries to raise funds for park maintenance. However, by 1918 the park was suffering financially and sold at public auction. Dane County acquired the park in 1935, renaming it Stewart Park in honor of long-time county board chairman Frank Stewart. Additional land was purchased to expand the park to its current 161 acres.

Stewart Park is located on County JG north of Mt. Horeb.

Pounding waves create spectacular rock formations at Cave Point Park.

Cave Point Park

Door County

The traveler's first impression of Cave Point is always one of majesty. Beautiful rock cliffs rise from the shore of Lake Michigan, which spreads, seemingly without end, to the horizon. Even on a calm day, waves hurl themselves against the cliffs, creating a thunderous noise. One cannot help but be awed by the power of the water and the strength of the rock.

Cave Point Park is a paradise for painters and photographers, and has been featured in numerous travel guides. Delicate ferns grow in rock crevices. Gnarled cedar trees hang over the cliff, their exposed roots clinging tenaciously to the rock. Holes in the cliff allow you to look down past moss-covered ledges to the water swirling below. The water itself is so clear you can see interestingly shaped rocks lying on the lake bed, and watch waves splash into underwater caves.

The rock formations at Cave Point consist of Niagara dolomite and are part of the Niagara Escarpment. Over time, the hard exterior layers of rock on the escarpment were washed away by Lake Michigan's powerful, persistent waves. The lake then cut into the soft inner rock, forming unusual shapes and crevices through erosion.

Land for the 18 ½-acre park was donated to Door County in 1943 and 1944 by the Hanson, Lyons and Reynolds families. Today, Cave Point County Park is surrounded by Whitefish Dunes State Park, which contains the highest sand dunes on the Wisconsin side of Lake Michigan. A short hike through a hardwood forest in the county park leads into the state park. Together, the parks illustrate the extremes of the Lake Michigan shore: sand dunes and rocky bluffs. Both parks are designed for day use only.

To reach Cave Point County Park, take County WD, off Highway 57, to Whitefish Dunes State Park and follow the signs.

Harstad Park

Eau Claire County

Harstad Park beckons us whenever we want to indulge in one of our favorite outdoor activities—canoeing. The park, which stretches along the banks of the Eau Claire River, contains 27 wooded campsites with easy river access. From here, canoeists can paddle downstream to another park—Big Falls County Park. Or you can paddle across the river to an 800-acre county forest, thick with oak, aspen, maple and white pine trees. The canoe landing is also a good spot for fishing, as it sits just below the point where Bridge Creek merges with the Eau Claire River. For canoeists, this all combines to make a unique and delightful camping experience.

The park attracts a wide variety of visitors. We particularly remember one visit, during which the youthful, boisterous banter of Boy Scouts was tempered by the serenity of an Amish family fishing from the riverbank near their horse and wagon.

The campground is considered primitive (pit toilets only), but it does accommodate trailers. Tall white pines form a natural screen between campsites. In other areas of the park, huge old oak trees arch majestically overhead.

Canoeists appreciate Harstad Park's river access, while picnickers relish the shade.

Land for Harstad Park was deeded to the county by Ole Harstad in 1932—thus the name. In addition to the campground and canoe landing, it contains a ballfield, playground and a large picnic shelter for day use.

Harstad Park is located on County HHH, which is off County HH southeast of Fall Creek.

Petrifying Springs Park

Kenosha County

Parks are especially important in southeastern Wisconsin, the state's most heavily populated region. Those of us who live here need places where we can get away from urban pressures, relax, and experience nature. If we did not set aside land for public parks, such places might cease to exist.

Petrifying Springs Park illustrates how distinct the separation between urban and natural environments can be. On an early-spring visit, we came upon the boundary of the park, next to which runs a heavily trafficked road. Because the trees were still bare, we could sense the movement of the cars racing by. Yet we knew that once the trees and shrubs leafed out, they would form a barrier that would completely block out this familiar urban distraction, leaving us with the feeling that we were surrounded by rural countryside.

Hiking trails at Petrifying Springs Park wind past unusual "contact" springs and the Pike River.

The park takes its name from springs on the park's south ravine, which were described as early as 1850. Called contact springs, they result when rainwater percolates through rock, hits an impervious layer, and then emerges from the hillside. The weakly acid water causes chemical changes in the soil. Sticks and other organic material become covered with lime. When the organic material decays, only this deposit, which resembles stone, remains. Because the organic matter does not become stone, this is not a true petrification process, but it appeared so to settlers.

Today, Petrifying Springs Park, which covers 360 acres, is an interesting mix of natural areas and modern recreational facilities. A collection of trees includes native species such as elms, oaks, hickories, aspens, maple and birches, along with varieties introduced by early settlers. The county's largest stand of white cedar, thought to be a remnant of the cold post-glacial period, dwells on the northwest ravine. The park also contains the county's largest black walnut, basswood and maple trees.

Recreational facilities include a hiking trail that meanders along the Pike River and past the petrifying springs, bridle paths for horseback riders and an 18-hole golf course. There are also picnic areas, several playgrounds, baseball diamonds, volleyball courts and horseshoe-pitching areas.

Petrifying Springs Park is located at the intersection of Highway 31 and County A north of Kenosha. (Access on summer weekends is via County JR, off Highway 31, at the south end of the park.)

Goose Island Park, in a magnificent setting on the Mississippi River, contains more than 400 campsites.

Goose Island Park

La Crosse County

Situated on an island in the Mississippi, Goose Island Park brings you close to a magnificent river and a host of natural wonders. Towering, rugged bluffs on the Minnesota bank form a scenic backdrop. Ducks and geese paddle through quiet sloughs. Eagles and egrets glide overhead. An abundance of fish drift through the waters—their size and quantity unequalled in the Midwest, local anglers say. Deer, fox, beaver, raccoons and muskrats roam the park too. On one visit, we and all other traffic came to a halt to allow a turtle to journey across the park road.

Covering 710 acres, Goose Island Park is one of the largest county parks in the state. More than 400 campsites accommodate all camping styles; there are electrical hookups for trailers, wooded tent sites and a primitive group camping area. Park amenities include showers, a store, boat and canoe rentals, and bait sales. Also available are basketball and volleyball courts, a swimming beach, playground, a new game room with video games and pool tables, five picnic shelters and five boat ramps.

A large part of Goose Island has been left undeveloped. Four hiking trails wander through a mixed hardwood forest of oak, walnut, locust, river birch and maple trees. A herd of about 100 deer live on the island and, since visitors feed them, are quite tame. Children love viewing the animals up close.

Goose Island was originally home to Native Americans, and Indian artifacts have been unearthed. The Army Corps of Engineers turned the land over to La Crosse County after it completed construction of the Mississippi's locks and dams.

Goose Island Park can be found on Highway 35 three miles south of the city of La Crosse.

Otter Lake Recreation Area

Lincoln County

We often wish we had discovered Otter Lake Recreation Area when we were a young family learning to camp. It's an ideal spot for introducing children to the joys of living outdoors. The rugged environment is perfect for tent camping and cooking over an open fire. Athough there is a boat landing, outboard motors are banned from Otter Lake. The quiet that results, combined with wooded shelters, creates an atmosphere of serenity and seclusion. The price is right too— $5 a night for camping in 1996.

You do have to drive two and a half miles down a gravel road to reach the park, but the destination is worth the dusty drive. Otter Lake is filled with enough bass and pan fish to satisfy any avid angler. Twenty-five campsites are clustered at one end of the lake; shoreline sites serve canoeists and boaters, or anyone who would like easy access to an early-morning dip. The day-use area contains a swimming beach, dressing rooms and a picnic area, which, set amid pine trees, also provides a feeling of seclusion. A hiking trail surrounds the lake.

Although the park itself is only 10 acres, it is situated within Lincoln County Forest, and other opportunities to explore Wisconsin's North Woods are nearby.

Secluded Otter Lake Recreation Area is a great spot for tent camping.

Half the camping sites are designated for trailers, but no electricity is available. Water is obtained from old-fashioned pumps.

To find Otter Lake Park, take County D east of Tomahawk, then go south on County H. Turn left onto Grundy Road, then left again onto Bear Trail Road. Follow Bear Trail to Otter Lake Road, which leads to the park entrance.

Cherney Maribel Caves Park

Manitowoc County

The first time we visited Cherney Maribel Caves we were on our way home from northern Wisconsin, looking for a place to stop and stretch our legs. We happened upon this miniature treasure, and it inspired us to begin our quest to tour all the county parks of Wisconsin.

Actually, our first impression of the park was that it was a good site for a picnic but nothing special. We soon found out that that is far from the truth. Spanning 75 acres along the West Twin River, Cherney Maribel Caves Park contains a lovely hiking trail, interesting rock formations, beautiful vegetation and, as its name reveals, caves.

Rugged wooden steps descend a steep slope and lead you to an isolated, almost untouched, woodland. In the spring, the wildflower display, especially of trilliums, is exceptional, and fall colors are outstanding. From here, you can walk along the riverbank and take in the beauty of the rippling water. Or you can hike next to the cliff face and enjoy the coolness of the moss-covered rock, moist with dripping water.

The cliff is a geologically significant feature of the park. In other areas of Wisconsin, glaciers covered the landscape with layers of boulder till. Here, glaciers scoured the land surface and exposed the underlying rock. It is this rock—called Niagara dolomite—that today forms the park's irregular cliffs. Water seeping through the rock from springs, along with freezing and thawing action, has broken down some of the cliff face and created caves. The smallest ones are merely holes in the bluff. A large cave is closed to the public, though it can be explored by qualified spelunkers; contact the Manitowoc County Parks office for permission. You can view the opening to the cave, blocked by doors, and an old

Lush vegetation hangs from the ledges at Cherney Maribel Caves Park.

wishing well from an observation platform. You can also see many enchanting springs along the hillside, surrounded in spring by rare ferns and wildflowers.

Even before Cherney Maribel Caves was acquired by the county, its natural beauty made it a popular gathering place. Picnics and even car races were held here. People tossed pennies into the wishing well and drew water from the springs. On private land just outside the park are the ruins of a stone structure that was once a bottling factory.

The park provides picnic tables, grills, a shelter, playground equipment and toilet facilities, making it perfect for family outings.

Cherney Maribel Caves Park is located on County R, east of Highway 43.

Dells of the Eau Claire Park

Marathon County

This park's major distinction is its view of the Dells of the Eau Claire River—walls of rock 30 to 40 feet high through which fast-moving water surges. For a mile and a half, the river tumbles, creating a cluster of mini-waterfalls. Huge boulders, nestled together, form pathways that beckon visitors to climb to the highest vantage points to view the spectacular sight. Young adults and agile children jump from rock to

Visitors scramble over the rocks to view the tumbling Eau Claire River at Dells of the Eau Claire Park.

rock along the bank, mimicking the movement of the free-flowing, frothy river. Other visitors sprawl atop sun-warmed rocks.

The dells' formation began more than two billion years ago when molten lava that was sprewed from volcanos hardened to form cliffs of mylonite rock. Over time, erosion and glacial movement wore down the cliffs, leaving a layer of volcanic rock. About 10,000 years ago, the last Wisconsin glacier carved the gorge that is seen today. The movement of the river through the gorge has since sculpted additional features, primarily "potholes," or smooth bowls as large as five feet in diameter gouged out by the swirling, wearing action of water and sand.

The 190-acre park is also noteworthy for its varied habitats in which many different kinds of plants—including rare ones—grow. Rock crevices along the riverbank are filled with ferns and mosses, hemlock and yellow birch trees. White and red pine dwell in a dry, windy zone along the top of the cliffs. A rich hardwood forest, comprised mostly of sugar maples, is found in the north end of the park. In April and May, it is carpeted with spring ephemerals—delicate wildflowers that appear before the trees leaf out. A prehistoric riverbed has been designated a State Scientific Area.

Recreational facilities include a stretch of the Ice Age Trail. There also are picnic tables, a shelter, playground and an excellent swimming beach (with dressing rooms) on a quiet stretch of the river. Twenty-six campsites accommodate tents and trailers. A group camping site is also available.

Dells of the Eau Claire Park is located east of Wausau on County Y, south of Highway 52.

Goodman Park

Marinette County

Every visit to Goodman Park reassures us that there is much beauty in this world to behold. It is so lovely that to visit it is to rejuvenate the soul. Goodman Park is worth going out of one's way to visit, and if we lived closer we surely would come here more often to soak in its quiet charm.

A perfect view of the Peshtigo River's rapids and waterfalls is the park's main attraction. Rushing waters tumble over rocks and boulders, split into small streams, then reunite into a large, flowing body of water. The action of the river is splendid, forming pools and brooklets of various sizes and creating islands of moss-covered rocks. Small trees lean over the water, their roots clinging precariously to the soil. All of this can be viewed from the riverbank or from two bridges that span the Peshtigo.

The 240-acre park is named after Robert B. Goodman, a lumberman and conservationist. Between 1936 and 1938, the Civilian Conservation Corps constructed two picturesque lodges of log and fieldstone that can be rented for day use. There is also a gazebo with a firepit for group picnics, and a playground for the kids. Even the restrooms are picturesque, built of the same log and stone as the other buildings.

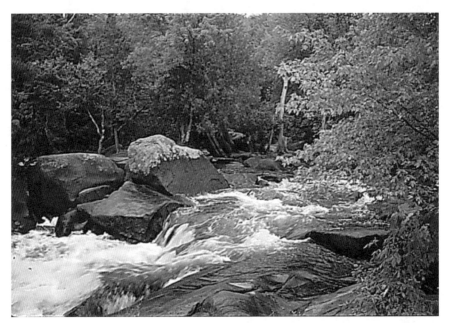

The wild Peshtigo River runs fast through Goodman Park, creating delightful rapids and waterfalls.

Twelve primitive campsites are nestled in a mature red pine plantation; a group site is also available. Trout fishing is good, and, although there is no formal swimming area, visitors have been known to jump into the larger pools of the river to cool off.

Goodman Park is located off Highway 8, 10 miles south of the town of Goodman. (Note: If Goodman Park campsites are full, you may want to try McClintock Park, which is two miles down the road.)

John Muir Memorial Park

Marquette County

Between 1849 and 1855, this site was the boyhood home of John Muir, who went on to found the Sierra Club and the national park system. Though he traveled all over the world, Muir never forgot this lovely spot, once remarking, "Even if I should never see it again, the beauty of its lilies and orchids is so pressed into my mind I shall always enjoy looking back on them in my imagination and even across seas and continents and perhaps after I am dead."

The "lilies and orchids" Muir remembered most likely grew in the fen—a wet grassland with unusual, sometimes rare, vegetation—that is found on the property. Hugh Iltis, professor of botany at the University of Wisconsin-Madison, first noticed the fen in the 1950s. On his recommendation, the site was designated a state natural area in 1972. Based on its historical and environmental significance, John Muir Park has also been declared a National Landmark.

A hiking path takes visitors around Ennis Lake past the fen and through a restored prairie in which grow New England asters, fringed gentians, blazing stars, nodding ladies tresses, golden alexanders and other native flowers. Canoeists and anglers can launch their craft from a boat landing. Picnic tables are available.

The 25-acre Ennis Lake is spring fed and extraordinarily deep for its size. Bessie Eggleston, a member of the Ennis family, which also owned land that is now part of the park, recalls that area residents had calculated the lake was "deeper than a ball of twine." A weight, she told us, was attached to a ball of twine and then dropped into the water. Although the ball completely unwound, the

Rare plants grow near Ennis Lake in John Muir Memorial Park, a designated National Landmark.

weighted end never touched bottom. Modern measurement methods reveal the lake to be 31 feet deep.

Because of hidden drop-offs, the lake was considered dangerous for swimming, and Eggleston remembers at least one drowning. As a child, she also was warned of snakes as large as stovepipes—a tale probably concocted to keep her away from the alluring but perilous water. The myth seemed true, however, after a daring boy killed a snake that was so long that when he slung it over his shoulders both ends touched the ground.

To preserve the park's fragile nature, access roads into it have been closed. But it is only a short walk from the parking lot to the natural areas. And walking is the most enjoyable, and fitting, way to experience this special site.

John Muir Memorial Park is north of Portage on County F, just north of the intersection with County O.

Grant Park

Milwaukee County

Grant Park holds some special memories. When Jeannette was a young Girl Scout, she visited the park with her troop very early one morning. A dense fog was rolling off Lake Michigan. As it ascended up the bluffs, it created a mystical image as delightful as any that could be produced in a Hollywood motion picture. And now, whenever she visits the park, she always recalls that magical morning.

But, among Milwaukee County's many outstanding parks, Grant Park is really a favorite for both of us. Not only does it bring back good memories, it contains a wonderful short hiking trail that spans the ravines between scenic bluffs that overlook the lake. The trail entrance is marked with a sign that says, appropriately: "Enter this wild wood and view the haunts of nature." From here, steps descend into a ravine through which a small brooklet trickles. The trail continues through a limestone gorge and a woodland forested with birch, beech and cedar trees, ending at the lake. You can continue along the beach for a mile and a half, next to the looming bluffs.

Grant Park contains other distinctive features, as well. Its 18-hole golf course was the first of its kind in the Milwaukee County Park system. The clubhouse, an 1892 Victorian farmhouse, is the former residence of the Fowle family, which

Grant Park features an 18-hole golf course and a clubhouse that was once a Victorian-era farmhouse.

sold the land that is now Grant Park to the county in 1910. You can also pedal along a portion of the '76' Bike Tour route, play tennis in any of six courts, picnic, and launch a boat. For those sturdy enough to tolerate the cold waters of Lake Michigan, there is a large, sandy beach with dressing rooms. Many children have had hours of fun sprawling here, building sandcastles and collecting the colored, fossil-filled stones that wash ashore.

Grant Park is located on Lake Drive in the city of South Milwaukee.

Whitnall Park

Milwaukee County

Charles B. Whitnall is often referred to as the "father" of Milwaukee's county parks. He planned Milwaukee County's park system and served on the Parks Commission from 1907 to 1947. Whitnall Park bears his name—a grand park to honor a grand man.

At 640 acres, it is the county's largest park and can best be described as several parks in one. One of its most notable features is Boerner Botanical Gardens, an internationally renowned horticultural showplace. Here, grass and gravel walkways lead visitors past perennial gardens, many filled with special seasonal groupings. Masses of tulips and daffodils open in spring. As summer progresses, a formal rose garden, with more than 4,500 plants, unfolds into bloom, along with beds full of irises and peonies. An herb garden shows off its plants in an ornamental display.

Shrubs and trees are highlighted too. More than a thousand crab apple trees of 250 species and cultivars represent the largest crab apple collection in the country. Stands of lilacs perfume the air. Connected to the formal gardens, a 1,000-acre arboretum harbors both native and nonnative trees and shrubs. A trial garden tests annuals, perennials, lawn grasses, fruit trees and even street trees for their suitability to the southern Wisconsin climate.

The Wehr Nature Center is also a vital part of Whitnall Park. Seven trails loop through various ecosystems in a 220-acre nature preserve. The nature center building houses interpretive exhibits.

Among the park's recreational facilities are an 18-hole golf course, a cross-

Enjoy outstanding floral displays at internationally renowned Boerner Botanical Gardens in Whitnall Park.

country ski trail and picnic areas with playgrounds. One of the latter offers climber-friendly trees, with lower branches close to the ground, on which children can test their skills.

Whitnall Park is in Hales Corners and can be entered either by heading west on Forest Home Avenue or south on Highway 100.

Plamann Park

Outagamie County

Plamann Park is an excellent example of an urban park, designed to offer a variety of natural and recreational experiences to city residents.

The 257-acre park, north of Appleton, contains a lush 90 acres of climax forest. Sugar maple trees predominate, and in May wildflowers offer a grand show. Area residents tell us that visitors flock

Spring wildflowers carpet the woods at Plamann Park.

here in spring just to see the blossoms. A self-guided nature trail provides information on the trees and plants.

In summer, a children's farm opens. Built to resemble a typical Wisconsin farm, it features calves, piglets, baby sheep, young goats and rabbits. Occasionally, more exotic animals, such as llamas, are in residence. Although the farm is not a petting zoo, children are able to observe the animals up close.

For recreation, Plamann Park has set up a novel, 27-hole disc golf course. This game is similar to golf, with players using Frisbees instead of golf balls and clubs. Use of the course is free. Other recreational facilities include a ballfield, volleyball and tennis courts, and a fitness course. There are also playgrounds and picnic areas.

Swimmers splash in a three-acre manmade lake. The beach is staffed with lifeguards, and dressing rooms are available. There is a modest charge to swim. Plamann Park is named for Robert S. Plamann, who donated the land for the park.

The park is off Ballard Road north of Appleton.

Covered Bridge Park preserves the last of Wisconsin's historic covered bridges.

Covered Bridge Park

Ozaukee County

Years ago, more than 40 covered bridges spanned Wisconsin's creeks and rivers. Today, only one remains—the Cedarburg Bridge in Ozaukee County. Here, it is easy to imagine horse-drawn wagons passing under the heavy beams, as light drifts through large, crisscrossing timbers that form the bridge walls.

The Cedarburg Bridge was built in 1876 at the request of area farmers who needed a sturdy, reliable crossing over Cedar Creek in order to transport their crops to market. Lumber for the bridge was cut and squared near Baraboo, then hauled to the site, where it was set in place according to a construction method known as "lattice truss." Interlacing 3- by 10-inch planks were held together by 2-inch hardwood pins; 3-inch planks were laid down for the floor. Lattice-truss structures are now very rare.

Why was a covered, rather than an open, bridge built? Various reasons are offered. Some say it sheltered travelers in storms. Others speculate that the roof protected the trusses. Or, the enclosed bridge may have been designed to keep oxen, who feared open water, from balking as they crossed over the creek. One theory (not a serious one, we assume!) is that the roof leveled off farmers' hayloads as they passed through.

Cedarburg Bridge was retired from active use in 1962. You can still walk through it, however. The small adjacent park, through which the Cedar Creek flows, contains a quiet and cozy picnic site. Enjoy lunch, stroll along the creek, read the historical marker, then step into the bridge and back in time.

Covered Bridge Park is on Covered Bridge Road, off Highway 143 north of Cedarburg.

Nugget Lake Park

Pierce County

Despite its name, nuggets of gold were never found in Nugget Lake Park. However, significant amounts of gold specks—"flour gold"—were discovered in Plum Creek, out of which Nugget Lake was formed, in the late 1800s. So were diamonds, some of gem quality.

Geologists had thought there would be bigger deposits. The broken and faulted bedrock in the area indicated that something had caused a significant disturbance. (The most accepted explanation is that a meteorite hit the earth here, leaving a deep crater.) The presence

Fishing and camping are outstanding at Nugget Lake Park, where gold specks and diamonds once were found.

of those faults, plus the discovery of the gold specks and diamonds in the creek, encouraged mining companies to do exploratory borings. But they found nothing, and pulled out of the area.

Nugget Lake Park encompasses 752 miles of semi-wilderness. You can still see the unusual faulted rock, called Blue Rock, in the northern section. The park is excellent for a camping vacation. There are 55 campsites (32 with electricity), showers and flush toilets. The 116-acre lake has a nice beach with dressing rooms and offers good fishing for bass and pan fish. Canoes and boats are available for rent. (Only electric trolling motors are allowed.) Seven miles of hiking trails are groomed for cross-country skiing in the winter.

Weekend nature programs, scheduled throughout the summer, are a notable feature. Nature films are also shown in an outdoor amphitheater. During the week, a naturalist is available by appointment for guided hikes.

The park charges a nominal entrance fee, in addition to a fee for overnight camping. It is located on County HH, two miles off County CC near Plum City.

Lake Emily Park

Portage County

Legend says that Lake Emily was named by an early settler to honor his beautiful wife. There certainly is no doubt about the loveliness of this setting. The large, glacially formed lake is filled with northern and walleye, and attracts ducks, geese, otters, muskrats and nesting sandhill cranes. Even bald eagles are occasionally seen gliding majestically overhead.

The park is unusually comprehensive. An enclosed area contains deer, turkeys and other wild animals, which kids love viewing up close. Indian burial mounds add to the park's historical significance.

Recreational facilities include a large sandy beach for summer swims, baseball fields, horseshoe-pitching areas and playgrounds.

The clear waters of Lake Emily attract sandhill cranes, otters, geese and bald eagles, as well as anglers.

Forty-nine campsites are tucked into a pine plantation. Of these, #49 is unique. For a $20 fee, the campsite comes prepared with a tent, screened shelter, cooler and lantern—perfect for novices not yet ready to invest in equipment or experienced campers who don't want to bother transporting their own gear. An additional attraction: This is the only campsite in the park that overlooks the lake.

Much of the land on which the park sits was once used to raise crops for the county home across the road. It was developed as a park in the 1940s.

Lake Emily Park is located off Highway 10, west of Amherst Junction.

For a panoramic view, climb the tower at Timm's Hill Park, the highest point in Wisconsin.

Timm's Hill Park

Price County

Fifteen thousand years ago, as the last Wisconsin glacier melted, boulders and other debris collected on top of the ice in some areas. In one case, this pile of debris was so high that it became the highest point in Wisconsin. It is called Timm's Hill.

As you drive to it, on a road that winds through a mixed hardwood forest, you can sense you are making a steep climb—to 1,951.5 feet above sea level, to be exact. To get a true appreciation for the height, however, you'll need to leave your car in the park's parking lot and continue a short way on foot. Follow the gravel path and then climb up the observation tower, and you will experience a great panoramic view over the surrounding forest's canopy of trees.

Timm's Hill park is a delightful spot for a picnic, and contains a newly constructed picnic shelter and a playground. Also within the 220-acre park lies all of Bass Lake and half of the shoreline of Timm's Hill Lake. You'll find a public pier on Bass Lake.

The park includes hiking trails and a connection to the Ice Age Trail. The forest of sugar maple, ash, basswood and birch puts on a spectacular show of color in autumn. (Color usually peaks the last two weeks of September.) In winter, the trails convert to exciting cross-country ski routes. One is even lighted for nighttime outings.

To reach Timm's Hill Park, take Highway 86 east of Ogema to County C south.

Pier Park

Richland County

A natural rock bridge is the center of attention at Pier Park. But why would a river run through a massive rock formation that rises 60 feet above the surrounding countryside? How could such an oddity have been formed?

Halsey Rinehart, who died five years ago, had made it his project to find out. His wife, Gyneth, shared the results of his research with us. She told us that the rock formation itself is made of blocked and layered sandstone and is very old, as this area of Wisconsin was not touched by the glacier that scoured the rest of the state. During a period of about 150 million years, streams meandered the floors of two separate valleys, one on each side of the rock formation. Coincidentally, they undercut the rock at about the same point, creating the natural bridge. The commingled streams now form the Pine River. Continued erosion, by water, wind and frost, further sculpted the rock.

A massive rock outcropping, undercut by a stream, highlights Pier Park.

The park was given to Richland County by the Pier family, and in 1922 a picnic area was developed. Unfortunately, after a flood in 1936, the park was neglected. A group of area residents, including Halsey Rinehart, lobbied for the park's protection and expansion, and in 1967 it became a county park. Mr. Rinehart and his son excavated a tunnel through the rock formation so that it can be viewed from both sides. Today, Pier Park contains picnic tables and a shelter, a playground and tent camping sites. A short hike to the top of the rock leads to a long, clear view of the beautiful Pine River Valley.

Pier Park is located on Highway 80 in the town of Rockbridge.

Magnolia Bluff Park

Rock County

We often schedule our parks trips for early spring. Parks are not as crowded, and, since the trees have not yet leafed out, rock formations and other landmarks are more visible. That's an especially good time to visit Magnolia Bluff.

Look for beautiful rock formations, grand vistas and challenging trails at Magnolia Bluff Park.

Though not quite the highest point in Rock County, it stands high above the countryside, and features beautiful rock outcroppings and grand vistas.

The scenery is a lovely backdrop for the picnic area that sits atop the bluff and helps create a relaxing atmosphere that is perfect for an outdoor meal. Grills are available for those wishing to cook.

Trails, some of them challenging, take hikers up and down the bluff, providing more vistas and close-up views of the rock formations. In the winter, the trails are available for cross-country skiing. Having hiked them, we concluded they would make for an exciting winter adventure, though not a recommended one for the novice or faint of heart.

A three-mile bridle path, formed with the assistance of the Tri-County Riders Club, is open to two-legged hoofers as well as horseback riders. (No motorized vehicles are allowed.)

Those interested in plants and animals should note that the north face of the bluff creates a special microclimate. Its cooler temperatures support a unique stand of white birch, a species not usually found growing so far south. It also attracts different birds and animals than the bluff's south face. Because of the two different microclimates, and the extreme changes in topography, the park harbors a very diverse number of birds and animals. The land for Magnolia Bluff Park was purchased in the 1960s; it was named for the township in which it is located.

You'll find Magnolia Bluff Park on Croak Road, off Highway 59.

Broughton Sheboygan Marsh Park

Sheboygan County

Broughton Sheboygan Marsh Park, part of a 13,000-acre wilderness area, contains a restaurant, lodge and campground.

We first visited Broughton Sheboygan Marsh Park in late summer. Although the day was overcast and windy, we were able to get out our canoe and explore the marsh, where we saw yellow-headed blackbirds. It was fascinating to see these striking birds clinging to the tips of reeds and cattails. When we returned several years later, we were disappointed to find that the water had been drawn down, exposing the mud flats and making the channels shallow and difficult to navigate by canoe. Our attitude brightened when we found we could then watch shorebirds feeding on the insects and shell life that had become accessible.

Part of a 13,000-acre wilderness area, Broughton Sheboygan Marsh Park is outstanding for the opportunity it provides to observe wildlife. Birds are plentiful and, besides yellow-headed blackbirds, include herons, nesting ospreys, sandhill cranes and a host of other water birds. Deer, beaver, otter and muskrat also call the marsh home. The best access for close-up observation is by boat or canoe, and both craft are available here for rent.

The park also has a civilized side. Campers will find 64 sites, electrical hookups and showers. A restaurant serves breakfast, lunch and dinner (typically, sandwiches, burgers and salads). A lodge is available for community gatherings.

The park also contains fishing piers, a playground and volleyball courts. In winter, trails are groomed for snowmobiling and cross-country skiing.

Broughton Sheboygan Marsh Park is located at the junction of county highways J and P, west of Elkhart Lake.

A quiet lake and the refreshing scent of pine trees make Keller Park perfect for picnics.

Keller Park

Waupaca County

If you want to spend a day up North, a visit to Keller Park is sure to please. Its picturesque setting spans the shore of a clear lake, the water so still that it reflects nearby trees like a mirror. The air is touched with a refreshing pine scent. The wind moves among the trees making that special, sighing sound you seem to hear only in the northern half of Wisconsin. Sitting in this park next to the lake and taking in the sights, smells and sounds of a summer day is a perfect way to enjoy the outdoors.

Keller Lake is an impoundment of the South Branch of the Pigeon River. The park covers the lake's eastern shore. Picnicking is very secluded, with tables amply separated for privacy. Granite outcroppings dot the landscape. Granite also covers the bottom of the lake and is easily seen through the clear water. Various hardwood trees, along with hemlock and pine, grow in the surrounding forest.

Recreational facilities include a launch area for boats and canoes. (The fish population is primarily trout and pan fish.) While there is no official beach, visitors swim in the lake, and a changing house is provided. For those wanting more active recreation, there are volleyball and basketball courts, hiking trails and a playground.

One week in August every year, the park is devoted to a day camp for county residents who are disabled. Restrooms have been modified, though they may not meet all the needs of the handicapped. While camping is not ordinarily allowed in the park, during this week some attendees may camp overnight. The land for Keller Park, 26 acres, was donated by Paul Keller, after whom it is named.

The park is located on County G about two miles northeast of Big Falls.

Mount Morris Hills Park

Waushara County

Mount Morris Hills Park is a favorite because it provides a natural setting from which to view Wisconsin's beautiful, sprawling farmland. The 377-acre park, located atop a 300-foot hill, is the highest spot in the county. A pleasant wooded drive up the hill creates a sense of anticipation for what you will find at the summit. And once there, from various vantage points, you are treated to panoramas of farms, neatly plowed fields, sparkling lakes and white churches with tall steeples.

The slopes here are too steep for farming, so the park was developed in the early '70s to preserve the view. The first time we entered the park, we were immediately struck by the meticulous care it receives. The facilities were in excellent condition, and the grounds were notably clean, with no litter to mar their beauty. Grass was so neatly trimmed that even the leaves that had fallen from the trees seemed out of place.

Mount Morris Hills Park is for day use only, with picnic tables, a shelter, ballfield, playground and tennis courts. Although there are many parks with

An eye-filling vista of farms, lakes and fields awaits the visitor to Mount Morris Hills Park.

similar facilities, you are sure to find this one exceptional. Its panoramas are quintessential rural Wisconsin, and it is exhilarating to be atop this hill and merely to breathe in the clean country air. This is an ideal location for the picnicker, the artist, the meditator and even the napper who wants to slumber in the freshest of outdoor environments.

Mount Morris Hills Park is on County G, north of the town of Mount Morris.

Powers Bluff Park

Wood County

Our first visit to Powers Bluff Park was in winter. The park sits on a quartzite bluff that is the highest point in Wood County, and this bright sunny day it was a hub of activity. As we walked from the parking lot, we were thrilled by the sight and sounds of exuberant children. They were sliding down a long snow-covered slope on large black inner tubes, and having a great time. Some of the more cautious sliders sat in the tubes while others belly-flopped head-first on their slippery downward journey. Their return trip was aided by a rope tow, which pulled the happy sliders back to the top where they eagerly began another downhill tube ride.

The scenery on this winter day was outstanding. Snow had settled picturesquely on the park's rock outcroppings and the tree branches. We were happy to find a heated community building in which to warm up, and a small downhill ski slope.

When we returned in summer, we learned about the park's history from several signs. Three Indian tribes have occupied the land: Chippewa, Potawatomi and Winnebago. Just south of the park are natural bogs from which the tribes harvested cranberries for trade. Within the park are two Indian dance rings and two Indian cemeteries.

An interesting feature of Powers Bluff Park is the quartzite rock, visible in many outcroppings. This rock is a combination of sedimentary rock and volcanic material. It is very hard, and survived the glacial scouring to which this region was subjected.

Children love the winter tubing slope at Powers Bluff Park.

The original parcel for Powers Bluff Park was tax-delinquent land donated by the old lumbering town of Arpin in 1948. Additional land was purchased and some was donated. Seventy acres are in a designated state natural area. A self-guided nature trail runs through the forest, which contains a unique species of mountain maple along with other maples, oaks and bass trees.

Powers Bluff Park is off County E, southeast of Arpin.

Best
Parks for Special Uses

Nature centers provide excellent educational opportunities. They foster an appreciation for nature and teach children about the importance of protecting the environment. Nature centers also are a source of pleasure for those who love the outdoors and want to increase their knowledge of Wisconsin's natural resources.

One of the finest facilities is **Mosquito Hill Nature Center** in Outagamie County. The 400-acre site includes a 200-foot hill—an obvious presence in the surrounding farmland. Even though this region was scoured by glaciers, this peak remains because it is capped by hard dolomite rock, which protected the layers of sandstone below. The Wolf River twists through the land around the hill, and

For directions to the parks mentioned, please refer to the listings in the next section of this book.

Learn about nature or enjoy the view at Mosquito Hill Nature Center.

sometimes in spring, when meltwater surrounds the trees, the wetlands here seem to mimic the swampland of the Southern bayou.

The Overlook Trail winds to the top of Mosquito Hill. Though it appears steep, it can easily be traversed even by inexperienced hikers. On our early spring visit, flowers dotted the path, and, to our delight, grass snakes were waking up from hibernation. One very young visitor proudly showed us a red-bellied snake, not much larger than a night crawler, that he had found. After he released it, we watched it slowly crawl away into the oak leaves that covered the forest floor.

Several other trails lead visitors to different natural areas. The Succession Loop runs past an oxbow lake that was formed when a portion of the Wolf River was cut off. The Waterthrush Walkway circles a frog pond. One trail, the Wet Meadow Trail, is handicapped accessible.

Mosquito Hill Nature Center also contains a building with interpretive displays about the Wolf River and other nature subjects. A staff naturalist and other experts offer an extensive program of guided hikes and workshops on such topics as birdwatching, star-viewing and snowshoe-making. Snowshoes may be rented for winter outings.

It's well worth a trip at least once in every season to spend a day at Mosquito Hill. Bring a picnic lunch, a camera and binoculars. If you don't have binoculars, this very well-run center will lend you a pair. Mosquito Hill Nature Center is open to the public on Saturdays and Sundays from 10 a.m. to 3 p.m.; it is open on weekdays by reservation only. It is located east of New London on County S.

Of the other county parks with nature centers, **Ledge View Nature Center** in Calumet County is best known for its caves. There is also a restored prairie and a lookout tower. Staff naturalists offer workshops and organize special events. The West Shores Interpretive Center at **Barkhausen Waterfowl Preserve** in Brown County contains nine miles of trails that lead through forest, meadows and wetlands. Outdoor education sessions, family nature programs and naturalist-led hikes are available year-round. **Retzer Nature Center** in Waukesha County incorporates diverse habitats, hiking and nature trails, and a building with nature displays. Special events and public hikes are available.

Horseback Riding

Several county parks cater to horseback riders by providing bridle paths. But one that offers special facilities is **White Mound Park** in Sauk County. The park's 1,100 acres contain a campground designated specifically for use by campers with horses, with 12 campsites and rails to secure the animals. Seven miles of bridle paths twist through oak forests and scenic meadows. Since this is unglaciated terrain, equestrians are treated to hours of pleasurable riding through rolling hills and valleys.

In addition, White Mound Park has a sandy beach with dressing facilities and two diving boards at 110-acre White Mound Lake, created when a dam was built here in 1969. More than a hundred species of birds have been sighted in the park, including red-headed woodpeckers. Deer, opossums, white-tailed jack rabbits, cottontail rabbits, beavers, racoons, and red and flying squirrels all reside in the park as well. A self-guided nature trail acquaints visitors with the park's vegetation. A camping area for nonriders has 72 sites. Reservations are accepted in advance for both campgrounds. White Mound Park is located on County GG, west of Highway 23.

Five miles of bridle paths can be found in **Big Eau Pleine Park** in Marathon County. **Magnolia Bluff Park** in Rock County has three miles of bridle paths. In Waukesha County, **Menomonee Park** contains three miles and **Muskego Park** contains two miles of bridle paths. **Petrifying Springs Park** in Kenosha County has about one mile of horse trail.

White Mound Park goes the extra mile by providing special campsites for horseback riders.

Out-of-the-Way Camping

County parks provide many opportunities to camp without modern amenities. There are parks that are hard to get to and secluded, that do not have electrical hookups, contain only a small number of sites, and allow campers

You'll find secluded campsites in a number of county parks, including Twelve Foot Falls Park and Perch Lake Recreational Area.

to enjoy the quiet of nature. These are parks for those who wish to "get away from it all." They offer only the basics: water, fire rings and outhouses.

Our favorite such camping area is **Twelve Foot Falls Park** in Marinette County. It contains 12 rugged tent sites along the Pike River, which is known for its beauty and trout fishing. Here, you can set up camp near a waterfall and be lulled to sleep by the steady rhythm of the water. We cannot think of a more relaxing sound. A five-minute walk from the campground takes you to another, smaller falls—Eight Foot Falls. A longer hike, of about a mile, leads to a picturesque view of Eighteen Foot Falls. The entire park is surrounded by Marinette County Forest, imparting a sense of great seclusion. To get to Twelve Foot Falls Park, take Lily Road south of Highway 8 and follow the signs.

Another park that is perfect for those who just want to pitch a tent is **Perch Lake Recreational Area** in Rusk County. It is located in the Blue Hills, a part of the state that is not extensively developed. Only a few highways serve the area, and campers must travel gravel back roads to reach the campground. Perch Lake Campground has 16 rugged campsites situated in a hardwood stand on a hill overlooking the lake. A nature trail, the Blue Hills trail system and a segment of the Ice Age Trail are nearby. To reach Perch Lake Campground, take County O north of Bruce to Fire Lane Road.

Other favorite camping retreats are **Harstad Park** in Eau Claire County, with 27 wooded sites near the Eau Claire River; **Big Falls Park** in Price County, with four sites; and **Mooney Dam Park**, with 13 sites on the Eau Claire River in Douglas County.

Historic Sites

Many county parks incorporate historical markers that denote the history of the area in which they are located, but only a few protect a historical structure. One of these is **Colonel Heg Memorial Park** in Racine County. This 15-acre park, set amid oak trees, is dedicated to Colonel Hans Christian Heg, who was the highest-ranking officer from Wisconsin killed in the Civil War and a well-known local Norwegian.

In one corner of the park stands a large statue of the colonel and a plaque honoring the sacrifice of his life in the war. The park is also the site of the Heg Museum. Colonel Heg, along with other Norwegians, settled in what became the town of Norway. The museum commemorates the life of these early settlers with displays, photographs and memorabilia. It is open weekends and holidays from Memorial Day to early September.

The park contains three other buildings, as well. One is a log cabin, believed to have been built in 1837 by a squatter farmer prior to the arrival of the Norwegian settlers. It is filled with items that might have been used by

Colonel Heg Memorial Park honors Wisconsin's highest-ranking Civil War officer.

the original occupants. A farming museum holds displays of early farm implements. The 1847 home of Reverend and Mrs. Elling Eielson can be viewed from the outside. The Reverend Eielson was a famous itinerant lay preacher of Norwegian descent. Unfortunately, the home is in need of restoration and is not open to the public.

One weekend every June, Colonel Heg Memorial Park is the site of living history demonstrations related to the Civil War and the contributions of Norwegian homesteaders.

For picnickers, the park has tables and a shelter. A ball diamond and horseshoe pits are available for more active sports enthusiasts, and a large playground provides exercise for children. A county bicycling trail runs close to the park. Colonel Heg Memorial Park is located just south of Wind Lake, off Highway 36.

Another park that preserves a historic structure is **Covered Bridge Park** in Ozaukee County, the site of the last remaining covered bridge in Wisconsin. Of the parks with historical markers, one of the most memorable is **Brigham Park** in Dane County. It is named after Ebenezer Brigham, one of the first white settlers in the area, and sits atop a high hill that affords a magnificent view of the surrounding ridges and valleys. Information markers explain the cultural heritage and natural history of Dane County. Rustic camping is provided.

Bird Watching

A ccess to nature and the viewing of wildlife are among the major purposes of county parks. But while any park with a body of water can attract waterfowl, only a few consider this the primary feature of the park. **L.H. Barkhausen Waterfowl Preserve** in Brown County is the best example of a county facility developed to observe waterfowl. This 920-acre preserve provides a wonderful opportunity to see the birds that are attracted to the western shore of Lake Michigan's Green Bay.

We recall our visit well. It was late afternoon, and the interpretive building had closed for the day. There were no other cars in the parking lot, and the sun was low on the horizon. But, in spite of the coolness of the spring day, the weather was lovely and we went for a short walk.

We were immediately entertained by the numerous songbirds flying from tree to tree. Goldfinches were gathered at the bird feeders—a delightful sight for us novice birders. The birds flittering around the ponds produced melodies as lovely as that of any choir and as inspiring as music echoing in a cathedral. For a time, it seemed that the only thing to do was to stop and listen.

One of the other great sites at Barkhausen is the spectacular spring and fall show of migrating ducks, geese and swans. Barkhausen sits on the southern end of a vast wetland that is one of the most productive ecosystems in the Great Lakes region. The 920 acres here are used extensively by waterfowl for feeding and resting. Nine miles of hiking trails lead visitors through marshes, meadows and forests where birds and other wildlife can be viewed. Several study areas are provided where you can sit and observe. On our hike, we stopped at a small pond and were delighted to spy three turtles sunning themselves on a log. As we approached, they quickly slipped into the pond. We walked away, then looked back, and—as we had predicted—they clambered back onto their perch.

For those not wishing to walk, there is a short drive that goes past several bodies of water where we have seen stately cranes, along with ducks and geese. Barkhausen's nature center, the West Shore Interpretive Center, offers family programs and naturalist-led hikes.

Bird watchers will want to catch the annual migration of geese, ducks and swans through L.H. Barkhausen Waterfowl Preserve.

To reach L.H. Barkhausen Waterfowl Preserve, take Highway 41 north of Green Bay. Exit on County M (Lineville Road) and go east to County J (Lakeview Drive). Turn north on J and travel one-quarter mile to the park entrance.

Another park that provides hours of pleasurable bird watching is the **Bird Sanctuary** in Douglas County. This 35-acre wildlife area preserves a habitat known as a pine barrens. The mixture of grass savannah and jack pine is home to sharp-tail grouse and a host of other birds, including upland sandpipers, rough-legged hawks and clay-colored sparrows.

Folk Art

Seldom does the notion occur that parks might have been established for nurturing an appreciation for art. But one Wisconsin county park exhibits a genre referred to as "folk art"—art created by those without formal training.

Wisconsin Concrete Park in Price County is considered one of the country's best displays of folk art, containing more than 200 sculptures by Fred

Concrete Park is considered one of the country's best displays of folk art, with more than 200 sculptures by Fred Smith.

Smith. Smith began sculpting in 1948 after he retired from logging at the age of 65. He completed his work in 1964. A self-taught artist, he made his pieces by covering wire forms with concrete and decorating them with glass, wood, stone and mirrors. Some of his massive figures are of mythical and historical characters, such as Paul Bunyan and Abraham Lincoln. A few resemble real people that Smith knew. Other sculptures include the Statue of Liberty and a wagon pulled by a hitch of horses. Viewing them up close one can't help but marvel at Smith's ingenuity and admire the perseverance it took to produce this body of work. It's a delight to stand next to the figures and imitate their stance or chuckle at their exaggerated facial features.

After Smith's death in 1976, Wisconsin Concrete Park was purchased by the Kohler Foundation, which restored the site before gifting it to Price County. Thanks to their efforts, Smith's forest of amusing sculptures will entertain visitors for years to come.

Wisconsin Concrete Park is open year-round during daylight hours, but is best seen between May 15 and October 1. A 40-page history and tour guide is available for a fee from the Price County Forestry Department (715-339-6371). The park is located on Highway 13 south of Phillips.

Waterfalls

Though waterfalls in county parks tend to be smaller than those in our state parks, they are every bit as charming to sit near and listen to. One of the waterfalls that we find most fascinating is **Long Slide Falls** in Marinette County. We don't get to visit this northeast corner of Wisconsin very often, but every time we do we stop by Long Slide Falls Park.

The cascading water drops 50 feet at a very steep pitch, then spills into the Pemebonwon River, tumbling over rocks and boulders. Here, the force of the water is so strong and the river so wild that spray bounces up into the air, forming an ethereal mist. Light rays reflect off the droplets and create rainbows. One of the magnificent aspects of the park is that visitors can climb up and over the rocks along the shore to view the falls from different locations, or you can simply sit on a rock and contemplate the beauty that lies before you.

We have found a healthy growth of poison ivy in this park, so it is advisable to stay on the paths. Be prepared for a one-quarter mile hike from the parking lot to the falls. Also be aware that there are no restrooms, picnic tables or other facilities. Morgan Park, a few miles east of Long Slide Falls, does have both camping and day-use facilities. To reach Long Slide Falls Park, take Highway 141 north of Pembine, then turn east on Morgan Park Road and follow the signs.

Marinette County bills itself as the Waterfall Capital of Wisconsin. You'll find more falls in **Goodman Park**, **Veteran's Memorial Park**, **Twelve Foot Falls Park** and **Dave's Falls Park**. A small waterfall on the Big Rib River can be found in **Rib Falls Park** in Marathon County. **Big Falls Park** in Eau Claire County provides a view of falls from both sides of the Eau Claire River; the view from the south side is more impressive but requires a drive of about a mile on a rough gravel road.

Waterfalls cascade through numerous Marinette County parks. Long Slide Falls drops 50 feet.

Native American History

To understand our country's heritage, we must learn the history of Native Americans. In Washington County, **Lizard Mound Park** offers us a glimpse into the lives of some of the area's earliest inhabitants. This treasure, almost hidden in a stand of trees, contains effigy mounds—low earthworks usually in the shape of animals. They were built by Indians who lived here between 500 A.D. and

Discover effigy mounds built between 500 A.D. and 1200 A.D. in Lizard Mound Park.

1200 A.D. and then seem to have disappeared. While some speculate that the mound builders migrated to other areas or were assimilated into other tribes, no one really knows for sure what happened to them. Except for a few rare examples in adjoining states, effigy mounds are found only in Wisconsin.

Excavation of the mounds has showed that they were used as burial sites for one or two individuals and sometimes a dog. From artifacts unearthed from the mounds, archeologists have concluded that these prehistoric peoples produced pottery, knew how to weave cloth, and relied on hunting and fishing, rather than farming, for food. They lived in scattered bands that moved regularly from place to place but returned to the same locations every year.

A trail at Lizard Mound Park enables visitors to view 25 mounds. Many of the mounds are lineal or conical in shape. The most striking is in the shape of a lizard. There also are eight examples of panther mounds and two of birds. (Names of the animals were assigned by archeologists and there is no way to verify the accuracy of their descriptions.) As the path weaves through numerous woods filled with oak, beech, sugar maple and basswood trees, hikers will be pleased to discover that they are also on a nature trail, with signs posted describing the vegetation and the possible use of certain trees or plants by the Indians.

There are picnic tables and restroom facilities in the park. The nature trail does show some signs of vandalism, but still offers a wealth of information. Lizard Mound Park is located on County A, off Highway 144 northeast of West Bend.

Goose Island Park, a large park on an island in the Mississippi in La Crosse County, is on the site of a Native American village. Powers Bluff

Park in Wood County makes special note of the practices of the tribes from that area by marking the location of ceremonial dance rings and two Indian cemeteries.

Caving at Ledge View Nature Center is a fun—and muddy—experience.

Caving

Of all the activities that county parks provide, caving is the most novel. At **Ledge View Nature Center** in Calumet County, a naturalist will take you underground, a wonderful adventure guaranteed to make you feel like a curious child once again.

These guided trips, scheduled regularly on weekends at 1 p.m., are nothing like the sedate tours offered at larger, commercial caves around the state. When we signed up, we were told that going on the "easier" tour meant we could stand up most of the time. And we were instructed on the "three Ds of caving": dark, damp and dirty.

Flashlights in hand, we and about 30 other participants proceeded to Carolyn's Caverns. This cave was discovered in 1986 after a sinkhole was noted— a feature that often indicates the presence of a cave. A metal door was unlocked and we slowly climbed down a ladder into the cave. From there we crawled through a small opening and over a ridge into another room. To get out, some participants went back up the ladder. Others took the optional exit: a shimmy up a mud slope to another door leading outside. The task was easy for the youngsters and a challenge for adults, and should not be attempted by anyone who does not want to get covered with mud.

This tour also includes a visit to Montgomery's Cave, which was discovered sometime before the Civil War. Ledge View schedules a more rigorous tour as well, which explores Mother's Cave and requires participants to crawl on their bellies much of the time. Ledge View Nature Center is located on Short Road, off County G south of Chilton.

Cherney Maribel Caves Park in Manitowoc County also contains caves, but these are open only to experienced cavers with the permission of the county parks office.

Canoeing

Canoeing is one of our favorite outdoor activities, and as we visited county parks we always looked for appealing waters. Lake canoeing is an enjoyable family activity and a good way to access prime fishing spots. River canoeing allows you to add overnight camping to canoe travel. While any park with a body of water and a boat landing is canoeable, some places offer a better experience than others.

One good spot for lake canoeing is **McMullen Park** in Monroe County. The park is situated on 600 acres of Monroe County forest land. Wazeda Lake is small and quiet; no gasoline motors are permitted. There are 30 campsites with electricity and four sites without electricity for tent camping. On one visit we were fortunate to see wild lupines in bloom.

Another kind of canoe adventure involves camping while on a downstream voyage, and some county parks have facilities designed for canoe camping. **Harstad Park**, on the Eau Claire River in Eau Claire County, contains 27 campsites with easy river access. **Kennedy Park**, in Juneau County, has very rustic camping for those paddling the Lemonweir River. (The Vilas County forest has a number of sites for canoeists that enable paddlers to do multi-day trips. See the Vilas County listings in the next section for details.)

Those who wish a somewhat different kind of canoe outing should visit **Broughton Sheboygan Marsh Park**. Facilities here enable visitors to navigate a marsh that is teeming with wildlife—a perfect use for a canoe.

Paddle a quiet lake at McMullen Park or camp alongside good canoeing rivers at Harstad Park and Kennedy Park.

Family Camping

Now that our children are grown, we frequently reflect upon our many happy memories of times spent camping as a family. Most of our camping experiences took place in the Northern Highland/American Legion State Forest. It wasn't until we got involved in this project that we became aware of the many excellent facilities provided by county parks for family camping.

Camping is a popular, low-cost vacation, but different families require different settings. Some prefer homelike comforts and look for campgrounds that accommodate trailers. These usually provide electricity and contain a large number of sites, a dumping station and showers. Other families would rather get closer to nature and seek more rugged campgrounds. There are county parks to suit both sets of requirements.

Whether your style of camping is primitive or deluxe, there is a county park that will suit your family's needs.

All families, however, need places that provide a wide variety of things to do so that families can enjoy spending time together and children won't become bored. A body of water is essential for most families, for swimming and, for older children, fishing. But children like to engage in other activities too. Nothing can spoil a family vacation for parents more than to hear their children complain that "there's nothing to do." The parks we mention here were selected because they offer more than a place to pitch a tent.

Some of the parks already described in the first section of this book are great for family camping. **Goose Island Park**, on the Mississippi River in La Crosse County, provides many opportunities for exploration simply because of its vast size—710 acres. Along with 400 campsites, it has showers, boat rentals, ball courts, a swimming beach and a game room. Primitive camping is also available. **Dells of the Eau Claire Park** in Marathon County is smaller, with only 25 sites, but children love exploring the interesting rock formations. **Lake Emily Park** in Portage County has a baseball field, bicycle path and a deer park. **Nugget Lake Park** in Pierce County provides weekend nature programs and has an onsite naturalist who teaches young people about the park's ecology. **Otter Lake Recreation Area** in Lincoln County is geared for families that want to get away from civilization.

One park combines many of these features. **Jordan Park** in Portage County has 22 campsites designed to be secluded. The park also accommodates trailer camping and has electricity, showers and flush toilets. One site is reserved for the handicapped, and three primitive campsites are available for canoeists on Jordan Pond. The park contains a deer pen, an aviary, a nature center (open on weekends) with hands-on displays for kids, a self-guided nature trail and a prairie restoration. The remains of a hydroelectric plant, used to capture the power of the Plover River in years past, offer a history lesson. For active pursuits, there is a ball diamond, fitness trail and a small beach. Of course, fishing is possible in the pond. And even though the park feels like it's far from civilization, Stevens Point is close by, affording other kinds of entertainment if weather should turn bad.

Winter Sports

Winter in Wisconsin brings many opportunities to enjoy the outdoors. Cross-country skiing on a brisk winter day is both exhilarating and scenic, and many county parks groom their hiking trails for use by nordic skiers. Snowmobiling is another popular winter activity, and many county parks do have snowmobile trails that cross their boundaries.

Only a few county parks, however, offer downhill skiing. One is **Calumet Park** on the eastern shore of Lake Winnebago in Calumet County, which has three adult slopes and two beginner runs with three rope tows. Lessons and rental equipment are available, along with night skiing, a sledding hill and 3.5 miles of cross-country ski trails. A ski lodge sells refreshments. **Mount Morris Hills Park** in Waushara County has a ski hill that is managed by a private company.

One county park that is designed almost exclusively for winter sports is **Standing Rocks Park** in Portage County. Named for the large boulders that dot the area, it features five downhill ski slopes and three rope tows. Bear Lake, at the base of the slopes, grants skiers a pleasant view. Skiers can warm up in a lodge that has warm food and drinks for sale, and rent equipment from a ski shop. For nordic skiers, 16 kilometers of groomed cross-country ski trails, considered some of the best in southcentral Wisconsin, wind up and down the park's hills. Modest fees are charged for use of the rope tows and the cross-country trails.

In summer, hiking and mountain biking are allowed on the cross-country trails. (A fee is charged for mountain biking.) If you wish to visit the park in summer, however, you must park outside the entrance and walk or ride your bike to the trailhead.

Another park with great winter sports opportunities is **Powers Bluff Park** in Wood County, also described in the section on favorite county parks. There are downhill ski slopes, though when we visited they were not in operation. The most popular activity here is tubing. The park provides big inner tubes for sliding down a long hill. It also has a rope tow set up that pulls the inner tubes and their riders back up the hill. Children seem to get as much of a kick out of the uphill ride as the downhill. In fact, it looked like so much fun when we visited that, if we had been dressed for it, we might have tried the activity ourselves, despite our age! In addition to exciting recreation, Powers Bluff Park is lovely to look at in winter, with its picturesque rock outcroppings capped with snow.

Many county parks groom cross-country ski trails. Mt. Morris Hills Park, Calumet Park and Standing Rocks Park also have downhill slopes.

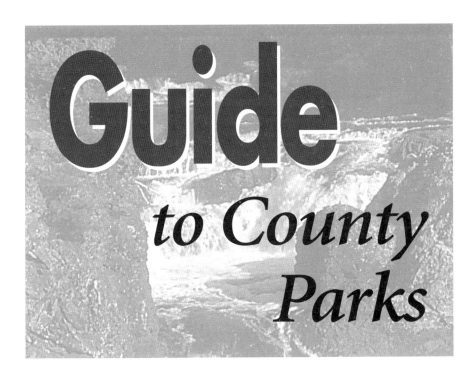

Guide
to County Parks

Contact: Adams County Park Department
Courthouse
Box 96
Friendship, WI 53934
(608) 339-4230

Big Roche-A-Cri Lake Public Access

Boat landing on Big Roche-A-Cri Lake.

Directions: Go north from Friendship on Highway 13 about five miles. Turn left on Cottonville Avenue and go west for two miles. Turn north on 13th Drive.

Facilities: Boat landing only.

55

Castle Rock Park

Located on the shores of Castle Rock Lake, Wisconsin's fourth largest inland lake, Castle Rock Park contains 200 open-field campsites. The lake is popular with water enthusiasts and anglers, and marked hiking trails wind through this scenic area.

Directions: Take Highway 13 to County F. Take County F west to County Z and go south one mile to the park.

Facilities: Picnic tables, picnic shelter, outhouses, toilets, tent sites, trailer sites, swimming, beach, dressing rooms, hiking, playground, boat landing.

Castle Rock Flowage Public Access (Birch's Landing)

Boat landing on Castle Rock Lake, with gas and oil available. Fish for northern pike, bass, walleye, pan fish and muskellunge.

Directions: From Friendship, go west on County J about six miles. Turn south on County Z and drive 1½ miles to the park.

Facilities: Boat landing only.

Crooked Lake Public Access

Boat landing on Crooked Lake. Fish for northern pike, bass and pan fish.

Directions: From the intersection of Highway 13 and Highway 82, go west on Highway 82 to 1st Avenue. Drive south ¼ mile on 1st Avenue.

Facilities: Boat landing only.

Deep Lake Public Access

Primitive boat landing on Deep Lake. Fish for bass and pan fish.

Directions: From the intersection of Highway 13 and Highway 82, take Highway 82 to County G. Go north ¼ mile on County G to the park.

Facilities: Boat landing only.

Easton Pond Park

Boat landing on Easton Pond, where anglers will find northern pike, bass, pan fish and trout.

Directions: From Friendship, take Highway 13 south to County A. Go ½ mile east on County A to 11th Drive and turn north.

Facilities: Boat landing only.

Fawn Lake Public Access

Boat landing on Fawn Lake. Fish for bass and trout.

Directions: From the intersection of Highway 13 and Highway 82, go south on Highway 13 about five miles. Turn left on 13th Avenue.

Facilities: Boat landing only.

Jordan Lake Public Access

Boat landing on the northwest end of Jordan Lake, where anglers will find northern pike, bass and pan fish.

Directions: From the intersection of Highway 13 and Highway 82, go east on Highway 82 nine miles. Go south on County G 2¼ miles to the park.

Facilities: Outhouses, boat landing.

Lake Arrowhead Park

This 300-acre lake is the site of weekly Saturday night waterski shows during the summer months. Picnic at the lakeside, launch a boat, or lounge on the beach.

Directions: From the town of Rome, take Highway 13 north to County D. Go west on County D 2½ miles to 15th Avenue and go south ½ mile to the park.

Facilities: Picnic tables, picnic shelter, outhouses, swimming, beach, playground, boat landing.

Lake Camelot Park

Anglers will appreciate the bass, northern pike, walleye and pan fish in this 445-acre lake located in the town of Rome. Swimming, boating and waterskiing are also popular activities during the summer months.

Directions: Go south 1½ miles on Highway 13 from the town of Rome. Go east on Apache Avenue to 10th Avenue, then drive north ¼ mile on 10th Avenue.

Facilities: Picnic tables, outhouses, swimming, beach, boat landing.

Lake Mason Park

Boat landing on 855-acre Lake Mason in the town of New Haven. Fish for northern pike, bass, walleye and pan fish.

Directions: From Briggsville, take Highway 23 west two miles. The park is on the right.

Facilities: Outhouses, boat landing.

Lake Sherwood Public Access

The smallest of three lakes in the town of Rome, Lake Sherwood attracts anglers for its bass, northern pike, walleye and pan fish. Waterskiers and boaters also can use the lake.

Directions: Take Highway 13 1½ miles south of the town of Rome. The park is on the left.

Facilities: Outhouses, boat landing.

McGinnis Lake Public Access

A spot to rest or fish for bass and pan fish on 33-acre McGinnis Lake in the town of New Chester.

Directions: Take Highway 82 to County G and turn north. The park is about six miles north on the left.

Facilities: None.

Patricks Lake Park

Formerly a 4-H camp, Patricks Lake County Park now receives little use except by area residents. Its isolated location makes it somewhat difficult to find, but the park offers a quiet spot for picnicking, and provides a swimming beach, playground and a boat landing.

County parks are a natural playground for children.

Directions: From Friendship, take Highway 13 south to County E. Go east on County E to Eagle Drive.

Facilities: Picnic tables, picnic shelter, outhouses, swimming, beach, baseball, playground, boat landing.

Petenwell Park

One of the largest county parks in Wisconsin, Petenwell Park encompasses more than 400 acres and 500 campsites. A marked hiking trail, swimming beach on 23,000-acre Petenwell Lake and cross-country ski trails provide recreation opportunities for every season.

Directions: From Friendship, go nine miles north on Highway 13 to County C. Go west on County C 6½ miles. Turn north on County Z, and left on Bighorn Drive.

Facilities: Picnic tables, picnic shelter, outhouses, toilets, tent sites, trailer sites, swimming, beach, dressing rooms, hiking, nature trails, cross-country skiing, playground, boat landing.

ASHLAND COUNTY

There are no county parks in Ashland County.

BARRON COUNTY

Contact: Barron County Recreation
1418 LaSalle Ave.
Barron, WI 54812
(715) 537-6295

A & I Park

The most developed of six canoe launch sites along the Red Cedar River, A & I Park is a place to picnic and to take a break from paddling. This spot is also known for its excellent smallmouth bass fishing.

Directions: From Highway 53, take the Chetek exit. Turn west on County I and travel 5½ miles to County A. Continue ¾ mile on the combination of County I and County A. The park will be just east of the Red Cedar River bridge.

Facilities: Picnic tables, outhouses, boat landing.

Angler's Park

Cast your line here for walleye and pan fish in this day-use park developed specifically for shore anglers. The fishing pier is handicapped accessible.

Directions: From the city of Chetek, follow County SS one mile north to the junction with County D. Follow County D through the intersection with County M for one mile to the west end of the Pokegama Lake bridge.

Facilities: Picnic tables, outhouses, boat landing.

Desair Lake Boat Landing

Boat landing on Desair Lake.

Directions: Exit Highway 53 onto Highway 48. Take Highway 48 1¼ miles to 18th Street. Then turn north and continue 2¼ miles to 23¼ Avenue. Travel east ¼ mile to the landing.

Facilities: Boat landing only.

Grant Park

Silver Lake's fine sand and clear waters make Grant Park a popular swimming spot. Other day-use activities include baseball, volleyball, a playground and picnicking.

Directions: Exit Highway 53 onto Highway 48. Go west three miles to County V. Turn north and continue four miles to County B. Go west 4¼ miles to the park.

Facilities: Picnic tables, picnic shelter, outhouses, swimming, beach, baseball, volleyball, playground, boat landing.

Kirby Lake Boat Landing

Though primarily used for lake access, walk-in camping is available for the primitive camper. Kirby Lake, known for its excellent supply of pan fish, is fished year-round. You can find the whole town ice fishing here on a good winter day.

Directions: From the junction of Highway 63 and Highway 48 in Cumberland, travel 4½ miles north on Highway 63 to 26½ Avenue. Turn west and go two miles to 4th Street. Turn north and proceed ¾ mile to 27¼ Avenue. Turn east and continue to the landing.

Facilities: Picnic tables, outhouses, tent sites, boat landing.

Southworth Memorial Park

Located on the Chetek chain of lakes, noted for excellent fishing, Southworth Memorial park offers camping in a more residential setting.

Directions: Exit Highway 53 at Chetek. Travel east on County I to County SS. Turn south and go 1½ miles to 6th Avenue. Then turn east and go 1½ miles to 26½ Street. Turn north and go ¼ mile to 5½ - 7 Street. Go west ½ mile to the park.

Facilities: Picnic tables, outhouses, tent sites, trailer sites, swimming, playground, boat landing.

Veterans Memorial Park

Pitch a tent or park a trailer in one of 30 wooded sites in the most quiet campground in Barron County. The park is located on Prairie Lake, part of the Chetek chain of lakes, noted for excellent fishing.

Directions: Exit onto Highway 8 from Highway 53. Travel east one mile to the junction with County SS. Turn south and go ¾ mile to 12¾ Avenue. Then turn east and go ¾ mile.

Facilities: Picnic tables, picnic shelter, outhouses, tent sites, trailer sites, swimming, hiking, nature trails, playground, boat landing.

Waldo Carlson Park

Anglers flock to this park to fish Red Cedar Lake, known as the top walleye lake in Barron County. Twenty-three sites are available for campers.

Directions: Exit Highway 53 onto Highway 48 in Rice Lake. Travel east for 13 miles to 29th Avenue. Turn east and go ¼ mile to the park.

Facilities: Picnic tables, outhouses, tent sites, trailer sites, boat landing.

BAYFIELD COUNTY

Contact: Bayfield County Tourism and Recreation
117 East Sixth St.
Courthouse
Box 832
Washburn, WI 54891
(800) GRAND FUN or (800) 472-6338

Atkins Lake Park

Located on the northeast corner of Atkins Lake, this park is popular with area residents. It is noted for its good swimming beach, fishing and boat-watching.

Directions: Take Highway 63 to County D. Go south on County D to Club Lake Road. Follow Club Lake Road southeast to the park.

Facilities: Picnic tables, outhouses, swimming, beach, boat landing.

Big Rock Park

Big Rock County Park is located on the Sioux River, a first-class steelhead trout stream. The park generates heavy bank and stream fishing and offers a spot for picnicking, wildlife viewing, hiking and rugged camping.

Directions: Take Highway 13 to County C in Washburn. Go three miles on County C to Big Rock Road. The park is 1½ miles down the road.

Facilities: Picnic tables, outhouses, tent sites, trailer sites, hiking, nature trails.

Delta Lake Park & Campground

An excellent fishing lake year-round, Delta Lake is stocked with northern pike, bass, perch, bluegill, crappie and bullhead. The park features bicycle trails, grills and 30 campsites equipped with electricity.

Directions: Take Highway 2 to County H. Go seven miles south on County H to Scenic Drive Road. The park entrance is about five miles down the road.

Facilities: Tent sites, trailer sites, swimming, beach, boat landing.

Twin Bear Campground & Park

Surrounded by oak, birch, maple and scattered pine, the campground and park are completely handicapped accessible. The northern pike, walleye, largemouth bass and bluegill make Twin Bear Lake popular with anglers.

Directions: Take Highway 2 to County H. Go south on County H for seven miles to the park.

Facilities: Picnic tables, outhouses, tent sites, trailer sites, swimming, boat landing.

BROWN COUNTY

Contact: Brown County Park Department
305 East Walnut
P.O. Box 23600
Green Bay, WI 54305-3600
(414) 448-4466

Bay Shore Park

Situated atop the bluffs along the eastern shore of the bay of Green Bay, Bay Shore Park is a popular family picnic and camping site. Hiking trails along the bluff lead down to the water's edge where you can launch a boat, fish, or swim. Campers choose from 100 sites; showers are available.

   Directions: From Green Bay, go north on Highway 57 for 11 miles.

   Facilities: Picnic tables, picnic shelter, toilets, tent sites, trailer sites, hiking, baseball, volleyball, playground, boat landing.

Brown County Fairgrounds

Home of the Brown County Fair during the month of August, the Brown County Fairgrounds has 50 wooded campsites. A boat landing and dock area provide access to the Fox River.

   Directions: South of Green Bay, take Highway 41 to Highway 32. From 32, turn east on Parkview Road in DePere.

   Facilities: Picnic tables, toilets, tent sites, trailer sites, baseball, playground, boat landing.

Brown County Park

Formerly the county golf course, Brown County Park is now a quiet, wooded picnic spot on Duck Creek.

   Directions: From Green Bay, take Highway 54 west to the park.

   Facilities: Picnic tables, toilets.

Brown County Reforestation Camp

With more than 1,600 acres, the Reforestation Camp offers a wide variety of outdoor activities. The park receives heavy use during the winter months by cross-country skiers. Warmer weather activities include nature trail hiking, mountain biking, picnicking, visits to the NEW Zoo (a breeding and survival center for endangered species) and shooting at the rifle range.

   Directions: Go north from Green Bay on Highway 41-141 to County B. Take County B west to County IR (Reforestation Road).

   Facilities: Picnic tables, picnic shelters, toilets, hiking, nature trails, cross-country skiing, baseball, volleyball, playground.

L.H. Barkhausen Waterfowl Preserve and Fort Howard Paper Foundation Wildlife Area

More than eight miles of hiking and cross-country ski trails wind through the wetlands, meadows and forests of this preserve. Thousands of ducks, geese and swans use the area for feeding and resting during their migration each spring and autumn. Interpretive programs and outdoor workshops with naturalists are available through the Interpretive Center.

Directions: From Green Bay, take Highway 41-141 north to Lineville Road. Go east on Lineville Road to County J (Lakeview Drive) and go north on County J one-half mile.

Facilities: Picnic tables, toilets, hiking, nature trails, cross-country skiing.

Lily Lake Park

Formed during the Ice Age, 40-acre Lily Lake offers wilderness-lined shores and abundant bass and crappie for the angler. A large dock and boat ramp is provided for motorized and nonmotorized boats.

Directions: From Green Bay, go east on Highway 29 to Lily Lake Road. Go south on Lily Lake Road.

Facilities: Picnic tables, outhouses, nature trails, playground, boat landing.

Neshota Park

Set in a river bottom, Neshota Park's scenery includes steep valleys and wooded hills. The park provides hiking opportunities, fishing in the Neshota River, a three-mile bridle path and, in the winter months, sledding, snowmobiling and cross-country skiing.

Directions: From Green Bay, take Highway 29 east to County T and go south. Go east on Park Road.

Facilities: Picnic tables, picnic shelter, toilets, hiking, cross-country skiing, volleyball, playground.

Pamperin Park

The largest developed park in Brown County, Pamperin Park provides large picnic and playground areas. Take a walk along the slow-flowing Duck Creek and over its historic suspension bridge.

Directions: Take Highway 29-32 to Shawano Avenue in the village of Howard. Go north on Shawano Avenue.

Facilities: Picnic tables, picnic shelter, toilets, baseball, volleyball, playground.

Suamico River Boat Access

This boat landing near the mouth of the Suamico River is a popular spot for shore fishing in summer and ice fishing in the winter. It also provides snowmobile access onto the bay of Green Bay.

Directions: From Highway 41 go east on County B (Sunset Beach Road) to the landing.
Facilities: Toilets, boat landing.

Way-Morr Park

Way-Morr Park offers summer-only picnicking and family recreation in a quiet, rural setting just south of Green Bay. The Branch River flows through the middle of the park.
Directions: Take County G south from DePere 12 miles.
Facilities: Picnic tables, picnic shelter, toilets, baseball, tennis, playground.

Wequiock Falls Park

Though it's the smallest park in Brown County, a large ravine here features the Wequiock Cascades, a 30-foot Niagara Escarpment rock formation. The falls flows freely in the spring and slows through the dry summer season, eventually freezing in a multicolored ice formation in the winter.
Directions: From Green Bay, go north on Highway 57 five miles.
Facilities: Picnic tables, toilets.

Wrightstown Park

This small park overlooks and provides access to the historic Fox River. Fish from the shore, launch your boat, or picnic near the scenic bluff.
Directions: Take Highway 96 to County ZZ (Washington Street) and go south into the village of Wrightstown.
Facilities: Picnic tables, picnic shelter, outhouses, playground, boat landing.

BUFFALO COUNTY

There are no county parks in Buffalo County.

BURNETT COUNTY

Contact: Burnett County Forest and Parks
7410 County K, #106
Siren, WI 54872
(715) 349-2157

Clam Dam Park

Located between Siren and Webster, Clam Dam Park provides canoe access to the Clam River. Fish from one of the benches along the river, or enjoy a picnic in the picnic area equipped with outdoor grills.

Directions: Take Highway 35 north of Siren to Krueger Road, go one mile to Pike Bend Road and turn left. Take Pike Bend Road to South Dam Road.

Facilities: Picnic tables, picnic shelter, outhouses, boat landing.

Clam Flowage Access

Boat landing on the east side of the Clam Flowage.

Directions: From Danbury, take County F west to South River Road. Go south 1½ miles to Cutler Road, then west ½ mile.

Facilities: Outhouses, boat landing.

Deer Lake Access

Boat landing on the west shore of Deer Lake.

Directions: Take Highway 77 east to West Deer Lake Road and go north about one mile.

Facilities: Picnic table, boat landing.

Devils Lake Beach

Spend a day at the beach or boating on Devils Lake, located northeast of Webster. The boat landing is handicapped accessible.

Directions: From Webster, take Highway 35 north to County C. Go east on County C to Devils Lake Road.

Facilities: Outhouses, swimming, beach, dressing rooms, boat landing.

Eagle Lake Access

Boat landing located on Look Creek, downstream from Eagle Lake. Access is for canoes and small boats only.

Directions: From Danbury, take Highway 35 north to Lake 26 Road. Take Lake 26 Road to Eagle Lake Road and go south (turn right).

Facilities: Boat landing only.

Godfrey Lake Access

Steep boat landing on Godfrey Lake, suitable for canoes and small boats.

Directions: Take Highway 35 just north of Polk County to Godfrey Lake Road and go east two miles.

Facilities: Boat landing only.

Jefferies Landing

Though primarily a boat access to Yellow Lake, Jefferies Landing is also adjacent to the Gandy Dancer Trail, the 90-mile limestone-surfaced bicycle trail that runs from St. Croix Falls to Superior. Picnic tables and grills are provided.

Directions: Take Highway 35 two miles north of Webster to Jefferies Road.
Facilities: Picnic tables, outhouses, boat landing.

Lake 26 Park

This out-of-the-way park, east of Danbury and somewhat difficult to find, features a 20-station nature trail. A boat landing and handicapped-accessible dock provide access to Lake 26. Outdoor grills are available in the picnic area.

Directions: Take Highway 35 north from Danbury to Lake 26 Road. Go east past Eagle Lake Road to Elliot Johnson Road and go south (turn right).
Facilities: Picnic tables, outhouses, swimming, beach, nature trails, boat landing.

Little McGraw Lake Access

Boat landing on Little McGraw Lake, limited to canoes and small boats.

Directions: Take Highway 35 north from Danbury across the St. Croix River. Turn right on St. Croix Trail and go 2½ miles to the access.
Facilities: Boat landing only.

Mallard Lake Access

Boat landing on the southeast shore of Mallard Lake.

Directions: From Siren, go north on Highway 35 to Highway 70. Take Highway 70 east to County X. Take County X to Emerson Road and go north (turn right) 1¾ miles to Gaslyn Road. Turn right on Gaslyn Road, right again on Mallard Cut-Across Road, and right again on Landing Road.
Facilities: Boat landing only.

Meenon Park

Picnic in a stone and log shelter built in the late 1930s by the Works Progress Administration. The park also features outdoor grills, a wheelchair-accessible picnic table and outhouse, and canoe access to the Clam River.

Directions: Take Highway 35 north from Siren. Signs indicate the exit to Meenon County Park, located on the east side of Highway 35.
Facilities: Picnic tables, picnic shelter, outhouses, boat landing.

Ralph Larrabee Park

Located on the northeast shore of Round Lake, Ralph Larrabee Park was donated to the county so that families could enjoy a natural swimming beach. The park is adjacent to the Gandy Dancer Trail.

Directions: From Danbury, take Highway 35 south to Round Lake Road and go about 200 yards.
Facilities: Swimming, beach.

Ray and Evelyn Pardun Memorial Access

Boat landing on the Yellow River, suitable for canoes.
Directions: Take Highway 35 north from Webster to Glendenning Road and turn left.
Facilities: Boat landing only.

Thoreson American Legion Park

Located on Wood Lake, Thoreson American Legion Park's picnic area includes a grill, picnic shelter and a wheelchair-accessible picnic table. A boat landing provides access to the lake.
Directions: Take Highway 70 to County Y and go south two miles.
Facilities: Picnic tables, picnic shelter, outhouses, dressing rooms, playground, boat landing.

Yellow Lake Narrows

Located between Big and Little Yellow Lakes, this park provides fishing benches and boat access to both lakes.
Directions: From Webster, take Highway 35 north to County U. Go 2½ miles on County U to North Lake Road and then south to Park Street. Turn right on Park Street and go ½ mile to Yellow Lake Road. Turn left.
Facilities: Picnic tables, boat landing.

CALUMET COUNTY

Contact: Calumet County Park
N6150 County EE
Hilbert, WI 54129
(414) 439-1008

Calumet County Park

Located on the eastern shore of Lake Winnebago, Calumet County Park features six panther-shaped Indian effigy mounds, ranging in size from 100 to 320 feet, and a portion of the Niagara Escarpment. Campers can choose from 71 campsites situated on the lakefront and nestled in the woods, 49 with electricity. Showers are available. Anglers will appreciate Lake Winnebago, stocked with the largest population of lake sturgeon in North America. Winter activities include downhill and cross-country skiing, sledding, ice fishing and winter camping.

Directions: From Stockbridge, take Highway 55 north two miles to County EE. Go west two miles on EE.

Facilities: Picnic tables, outhouses, toilets, tent sites, trailer sites, swimming, beach, hiking, nature trails, cross-country skiing, volleyball, playground, boat landing.

Ledge View Nature Center

Those up for a physical challenge will want to explore the three caves at Ledge View Nature Center—crawling, crouching and squeezing is required. Visitors can also enjoy the wildflowers in the prairie, the lookout tower and nature trails.

Directions: Take County G south from Chilton to Short Road, on which Ledge View is located.

Facilities: Picnic tables, outhouses, hiking, nature trails.

CHIPPEWA COUNTY

Contact: Chippewa County Forest and Parks Department
Chippewa County Courthouse
711 North Bridge St.
Chippewa Falls, WI 54729-1876
(715) 726-7880

Morris-Erickson Park

Long Lake's crystal-clear waters make Morris-Erickson Park a popular spot for swimming, boating and fishing. Anglers will find and, with some luck, catch populations of walleye, smallmouth bass and muskellunge. (The clear waters make fishing challenging at times.) The park's 28 campsites, complete with electricity, face the lakefront.

Directions: Take Highway 40 north from Bloomer about 10 miles. The park is just off Highway 40.

Facilities: Picnic tables, outhouses, tent sites, trailer sites, swimming, beach, playground, boat landing.

Otter Lake Park

The most popular of the county's three parks, Otter Lake County Park offers 22 wooded sites for a rustic camping experience. Otter Lake is stocked with walleye, bass and pan fish for the fishing enthusiast and also offers a place to swim, boat, or just relax on the beach.

Directions: Take County G to 170th Avenue.
Facilities: Picnic tables, picnic shelter, outhouses, tent sites, trailer sites, swimming, beach, dressing rooms, nature trails, volleyball, playground, boat landing.

Pine Point Park

Pine Point County Park is on a peninsula, wooded throughout and surrounded by 3,900-acre Lake Holcombe. Some of the 48 campsites sit lakeside, offering scenic views of the flowage used for boating, swimming and fishing. Anglers will find an abundance of muskellunge, walleye, large and smallmouth bass, and catfish.
Directions: From Cornell, go north on Highway 27 to County M. Go east on County M for 2½ miles.
Facilities: Picnic tables, picnic shelter, outhouses, tent sites, trailer sites, swimming, beach, playground, boat landing.

CLARK COUNTY

Contact: Clark County Forestry and Parks Department
Courthouse
517 Court St.
Neillsville, WI 54456
(715) 743-5140

Black River Park

Fishing is the most popular activity at this day-use park on the Black River. Anglers will find large and smallmouth bass, bluegill and pan fish.
Directions: From Withee at junction of highways 29 and 37, go west on Highway 29 2½ miles to the park entrance.
Facilities: Picnic tables, picnic shelter, outhouses, playground.

Bruce Mound Winter Sports Area

Located just west of Neillsville, this park offers cold-weather weekend recreation. Slide down one of six inner-tubing chutes, ski beginner and intermediate hills, or explore marked cross-country ski trails. The park supplies the inner tubes, and downhill and cross-country ski equipment is available for rent. Visitors will appreciate the heated chalet with restrooms, concessions and a view of the outdoor activities.

Directions: From Neillsville, go southwest on Highway 95 15 miles to Bruce Mound Avenue. Go south on Bruce Mound Avenue ½ mile to the park entrance.
Facilities: Toilets, cross-country skiing.

Greenwood Park

A popular spot for family reunions and weddings, Greenwood County Park offers a scenic spot to picnic on the Black River. Camping is limited, with 14 open-field electric sites available. The Black River is populated with large and smallmouth bass, bluegill and pan fish.
Directions: From Greenwood, take Highway 73 north ½ mile.
Facilities: Picnic tables, picnic shelter, outhouses, tent sites, trailer sites, playground.

Humbird Park

Situated on Emerson Lake, Humbird County Park offers opportunities to swim, boat, fish and picnic. Anglers will find largemouth bass and pan fish.
Directions: Look for the park on the northwest edge of the village of Humbird, at the junction of Highway 12-27 and County B.
Facilities: Picnic tables, picnic shelter, outhouses, swimming, playground, boat landing.

Loyal Park

A day-use park in the town of Loyal, Loyal County Park has volleyball courts, horseshoe pits and a baseball diamond with bleachers, and is adjacent to a five-hole golf course.
Directions: The park is on the western edge of the city of Loyal, off Highway 98.
Facilities: Picnic tables, picnic shelter, outhouses, baseball, volleyball, playground.

Moraine Park

Moraine County Park contains picnic facilities and overlooks some of Wisconsin's most scenic woodlands and moraine areas. The park is adjacent to the Highground Veterans Memorial, a collection of metal sculptures and plantings paying tribute to all veterans of the 20th century.
Directions: From Neillsville, take Highway 10 west three miles to the park entrance.
Facilities: Picnic tables, picnic shelter, outhouses.

North Mead Lake Park

Its remote location on the 133,000-acre Clark County Forest land creates opportunities for a scenic drive or hike. The park has 71 campsites and access to Mead Lake, where visitors can swim at the beach, launch a boat, or fish for largemouth bass, pan fish, northern pike and muskellunge.

Directions: From Greenwood, take County G west three miles to County O. Go north on County O two miles to County MM. Take County MM west five miles to the park entrance.

Facilities: Picnic tables, picnic shelter, outhouses, tent sites, trailer sites, swimming, beach, dressing rooms, playground, boat landing.

Rock Dam Park

Campers will appreciate the amenities at Rock Dam County Park's 134-site campground, including grills, electricity, showers, concessions and laundromat. From here, hikers and cross-country skiers can access miles of trails that wind through the county forest just north of the park. Rock Dam Lake is filled with largemouth bass, northern pike and pan fish, and also provides a spot to swim, rest on its beaches, or launch a boat.

Directions: From Greenwood, take County G west eight miles to County GG. Go west on County GG six miles to the park entrance.

Facilities: Picnic tables, picnic shelter, outhouses, tent sites, trailer sites, swimming, beach, dressing rooms, playground, boat landing.

Russell Park

Located on Lake Arbutus in the southwestern corner of the county, Russell County Park offers campers 230 sites. All have electricity and some are handicapped accessible. Other amenities include showers, a laundromat and concessions. Three miles away is the Levis Mound Trail, where outdoor enthusiasts can hike, mountain bike, ride horseback, and cross-country ski through diverse terrain. Lake Arbutus is populated with largemouth bass, walleye, northern pike, muskellunge and pan fish.

Directions: From Neillsville, take Highway 95 southwest 12 miles to County J. Go south on County J three miles to the park entrance.

Facilities: Picnic tables, picnic shelter, outhouses, toilets, tent sites, trailer sites, swimming, beach, dressing rooms, volleyball, playground, boat landing.

Sherwood Park

A bit off the beaten path, this park offers a rustic camping environment. Its 27 remote sites are wooded and close to Sherwood Lake, which provides opportunities for swimming, boating and fishing for largemouth bass, northern pike and pan fish.

Directions: From Neillsville, take Highway 73 southeast 18 miles to County Z. Go south two miles on County Z to the park entrance.

Facilities: Picnic tables, picnic shelter, outhouses, tent sites, trailer sites, swimming, dressing rooms, playground, boat landing.

Snyder Park

Though it has been overhauled in the last two years, you will still find logs from the old lumber days as you wander through Snyder County Park. Visitors can swim, boat, and fish in Snyder Lake or go for a scenic hike along Wedges Creek. Thirty-five campsites, with electricity, are available, and, for snowmobilers, there is access to a nearby ATV trail.

Directions: From Neillsville, take Highway 10 west six miles to County B and turn right. Go one mile to the park entrance.

Facilities: Picnic tables, picnic shelter, outhouses, tent sites, trailer sites, swimming, beach, hiking, playground, boat landing.

South Mead Lake Park

Located just across the lake from North Mead Lake County Park, this day-use park offers a spot to picnic, launch a boat, and fish for largemouth bass, pan fish, northern pike and muskellunge. Its remote setting on Clark County Forest land creates opportunities for scenic hikes and drives.

Directions: From Greenwood, take County G west three miles to County O. Go north on County O two miles to County MM. Go west on County MM five miles to the park entrance.

Facilities: Picnic tables, picnic shelter, outhouses, playground, boat landing.

Wildcat Mound Park

Hike your way through Wildcat Mound County Park, known for its premiere scenic overlooks. Autumn visitors will enjoy the changing colors of the oak, maple, birch and aspen trees that cover the terrain.

Directions: From Neillsville, take Highway 10 west seven miles to County B. Go west on County B seven miles to the park entrance.

Facilities: Picnic tables, outhouses, hiking.

Wild Rock Park

Though there are no designated sites, adventurous campers can pitch a tent here. Firewood, grills and electricity are available. Wild Rock County Park provides access to hiking, bridle and snowmobile trails.

Directions: From Neillsville, take Highway 10 west three miles to County G. Go north 12 miles on County G to County I. Go west four miles on County I to the park entrance.

Facilities: Picnic tables, picnic shelter, outhouses, tent sites, hiking.

COLUMBIA COUNTY

Contact: Columbia County Highway Department
P.O. Box 875
Wyocena, WI 53969
(608) 429-2156

Governor's Bend Park

This is a nice little spot to stop for a picnic. The outhouses are handicapped accessible.

Directions: Take Highway 33 to County F. Go north three miles on County F and turn left on Fox River Road. Take Fox River Road to Lock Road and turn left again.

Facilities: Picnic tables, outhouses.

Highway 44 Wayside

Travelers can enjoy a picnic break at this wayside on Highway 44, on the edge of Park Lake. The lake is popular with water enthusiasts, who can launch a boat, waterski, swim, or fish. Anglers can expect to see northern pike, bass, bluegill, and crappie. Outhouses are handicapped accessible.

Directions: From Pardeeville, go ½ mile north on Highway 44.

Facilities: Picnic tables, outhouses, swimming, boat landing.

Lake George Park

Visitors can swim, launch their boats, and fish for bass and bluegill at this very small park. The outhouses are handicapped accessible.

Directions: Take Highway 51 north to County P. Go east two miles on County P, about ½ mile past West Bush Road.

Facilities: Outhouses, swimming, boat landing.

Owen Park

Picnic up high on a scenic hilltop. The outhouses are handicapped accessible.

Directions: Take Highway 78 five miles southwest of Highway 90-94 to Owen Park Road and turn right. Go 1½ miles to the park entrance.

Facilities: Picnic tables, outhouses.

Wyona Park

Anglers can fish off the bridge over Duck Creek for northern pike, bluegill and bass. The park also offers a place to launch a boat, a playground and a few picnic tables.

Directions: From Wyocena, go east on County G and take the first left, which is about ¼ mile down the road.

Facilities: Picnic tables, outhouses, playground, boat landing.

CRAWFORD COUNTY

Contact: Crawford County Highway Department
P.O. Box 265
Gays Mills, WI 54631
(608) 735-4300

Crowley Park

This small park on Crowley Ridge offers a quiet, remote spot for picnics. The site provides tables, a grill and a shelter.

Directions: From Prairie du Chien, take Highway 27 north to County E, just south of Seneca. Turn east on County E and travel four miles to the park.

Facilities: Picnic tables, picnic shelter.

Husher Park

Located on Highway 131 north of Wauzeka, Husher Park is a small wayside with an observation platform overlooking the Kickapoo River Valley. The scenic view makes this a pleasant spot for a picnic.

Directions: From Prairie du Chien, take Highway 35 east to Highway 60. Continue northeast on Highway 60 through Wauzeka. Just east of Wauzeka, turn north on Highway 131. Travel two miles to the park.

Facilities: Picnic tables.

DANE COUNTY

Contact: Dane County Park Commission
4318 Robertson Road
Madison, WI 53714
(608) 246-3896

Babcock Park

Located on Lake Waubesa near the village of McFarland, Babcock Park is a popular spot to launch a boat and spend the day fishing. The boat landing area offers a fish-cleaning facility. Twenty-five campsites are available, all supplied with electricity; showers also are available. Toilets, campsites and fishing facilities are all handicapped accessible.

Directions: Take Highway 51 north from the village of McFarland. Park on the east side of Highway 51.

Facilities: Picnic tables, picnic shelter, toilets, tent sites, trailer sites, playground, boat landing.

A naturalist at Pierce County's Nugget Lake Park teaches young people about the park's ecology.

Badger Prairie Park

Though one of Dane County's largest parks, most of Badger Prairie Park's 339 acres are currently undeveloped. Visitors can picnic or find recreation in one of several softball and soccer fields. The park also provides access to the Military Ridge State Trail, a bicycle trail from Madison to Dodgeville, and the National Ice Age Hiking Trail.

Directions: From Madison, take Highway 151 south to County PB. The park entrance is at this intersection.

Facilities: Picnic tables, picnic shelter, toilets, baseball, playground.

Brigham Park

Trek your way through the maple woods on a self-guided nature trail and enjoy a scenic view of northwestern Dane County at Brigham Park. Twenty-five rustic campsites are available; in the winter months, cross-country ski trails are marked.

> **Directions:** Take Highway 18-151 west to Blue Mounds. Turn right on County F.
> **Facilities:** Picnic tables, picnic shelter, outhouses, toilets, tent sites, trailer sites, hiking, nature trails, cross-country skiing, playground.

Cam-Rock Park

Bordered by the Koshkonong Creek, 300-acre Cam-Rock park offers trails for year-round hiking, seasonal cross-country skiing and mountain biking. A portion of the creek has become a refuge for migrating ducks and geese in the spring and fall. A trail and observation deck allow visitors to watch the birds.

> **Directions:** Go east on Highways 12 & 18 to County B.
> **Facilities:** Picnic tables, picnic shelter, outhouses, hiking, cross-country skiing.

Festge Park/Salmo Pond

Festge Park's 126 wooded acres are located within Wisconsin's driftless area. A 100-foot-high scenic overlook provides a view of the surrounding countryside. Visitors can enjoy a shaded picnic, a walk along the nature trail or fishing in Salmo Pond. The fishing pier is handicapped accessible.

> **Directions:** Take Highway 14 1¼ miles west of Cross Plains to Scherbel Road and turn right.
> **Facilities:** Picnic tables, picnic shelter, outhouses, nature trails, baseball, playground.

Fish Camp Launch

Located at the inlet of the Yahara River, Fish Camp Launch provides boat access to Lake Kegonsa. Visitors can sit lakeside for a picnic or cast a line for fish.

> **Directions:** Take Highway 51 to County AB. Take County AB to Fish Camp Road, which ends at the park.
> **Facilities:** Picnic tables, toilets, boat landing.

Fish Lake Park

This small park is located on 252-acre Fish Lake, where anglers will find northern pike, largemouth bass and pan fish. The park also offers a picnic area, playground and access to the lake for nonmotorized boats.

> **Directions:** Take Highway 12 to County KP. Go north on County KP and turn right onto County Y. From County Y, turn left at Mack Road and then right onto Fish Lake Road.
> **Facilities:** Picnic tables, picnic shelter, playground, boat landing.

Goodland Park

Located on the west shore of Lake Waubesa, Goodland Park offers several hundred feet of shoreline and various opportunities for outdoor recreation. Visitors can picnic, swim at the beach, and play volleyball, tennis, basketball and softball.

Directions: Take Highway 14 south from Madison to County MM. Turn off County MM at Goodland Park Road.

Facilities: Picnic tables, picnic shelter, outhouses, toilets, swimming, beach, baseball, volleyball, tennis, playground, boat landing.

Halfway Prairie

In operation from 1844 to 1961, Halfway Prairie School is the oldest rural elementary school in Dane County. Early miners used to camp nearby. Visitors can view the inside of the restored school on holidays and Sunday afternoons, 1 to 5 p.m., from Memorial Day through Labor Day.

Directions: Take Highway 12 to Highway 19. Go east on Highway 19 to its junction with County F, where the school is located, just north of the village of Black Earth.

Facilities: Picnic tables, outhouses, playground.

Holtzman Natural Resource Area

Access to this 64-acre nature conservancy and wildlife refuge can be obtained only by receiving permission from one of the surrounding private landowners. Contact the Dane County Park Commission office.

Directions: South side of Madison, east of Highway 14.

Facilities: None.

Indian Lake Park

A winding trail at 442-acre Indian Lake Park leads to a view of the lake and surrounding valley and a historic chapel built in 1857. The hilly park provides miles of cross-country ski and nature trails, including 900 feet of elevated boardwalk along one trail that circles the lake. Camping is available for groups only. Winter visitors have access to a log cabin warming house.

Directions: Take Highway 12 north to Highway 19 and turn left. Go four miles to the park entrance.

Facilities: Picnic tables, picnic shelter, outhouses, hiking, nature trails, cross-country skiing, boat landing.

La Follette Park

Located on the east shore of Lake Kegonsa at the outlet of the Yahara River, La Follette Park offers anglers a spot to shore fish on the locks and dam. Visitors can also launch a canoe here.

Directions: Take Highway 51 to County B. Go east on County B 1½ miles to Williams Drive and turn north.
Facilities: Picnic tables, picnic shelter, outhouses, beach, playground, boat landing.

Lake Farm Park

The Native American Archaeological Trail leads you past shoreline and through prairie land with informational markers describing the period from 10,000 B.C. to 300 A.D., when Native Americans lived in this area. The park can be used for cross-country skiing in the winter. Lake Farm Park also offers group campsites, picnic facilities and a handicapped-accessible boat landing.
Directions: Take Highway 18-151 to South Towne Drive. Go south on South Towne Drive to Moorland Road, east on Moorland Road to Libby Road.
Facilities: Picnic tables, picnic shelter, toilets, hiking, nature trails, cross-country skiing, baseball, volleyball, playground, boat landing.

Lakeview Woods

This heavily wooded 27-acre conservancy park is the highest point on the north side of Madison, offering a scenic view of Lake Mendota. Visitors can picnic and hike through the woods.
Directions: Take Highway 113 to Northport Drive in Madison.
Facilities: Picnic tables, hiking, nature trails.

Mendota Park

Mendota Park offers "urban" camping on Lake Mendota. Visitors can swim at the beach, launch a boat, or play a game of basketball or tennis. Thirty campsites, with electricity, and showers are available.
Directions: Take Highway 12-14 north to County M. Turn right and go 2½ miles on County M to the park entrance.
Facilities: Picnic tables, picnic shelter, toilets, tent sites, trailer sites, swimming, beach, dressing rooms, baseball, volleyball, tennis, playground, boat landing.

Nine Springs E-Way

Six miles of trail currently wind through this developing system of year-round nature trails. The E-Way extends from Dunn's Marsh to Lake Farm Park on Lake Waubesa and includes wetlands, sedge meadows, native forests and many large springs, which flow into Nine Springs Creek. The trails provide opportunities to jog, hike, study nature, and, in winter, cross-country ski.
Directions: To reach the trailhead at Lake Farm Park, take Highway 12-18 to South Towne Drive, go south on South Towne Drive to Moorland Road and go east to the parking area.
Facilities: Hiking, nature trails, cross-country skiing.

Phil's Woods

Walk through 37 acres of natural woods and meadow, named for former three-time governor of Wisconsin, Phillip La Follette. The Baraboo Bluffs and Sauk Prairie can be seen from the western field.

Directions: Take Highway 12 to Dunlap Hollow Road and go south 1¼ miles.
Facilities: Hiking, nature trails.

Riley-Deppe Park

Visitors can launch a boat onto the park's mill pond, fish along its shoreline, or relax with a quiet picnic.

Directions: Off Highway 19, on the west edge of the village of Marshall.
Facilities: Picnic tables, picnic shelter, outhouses, playground, boat landing.

Schumacher Farm

More than 100 native plant species grow within this 10-acre prairie donated to the public for development as an open-air museum. Schumacher Trail winds through a variety of tall-grass prairie plants.

Directions: From Madison, take Highway 113-19 northwest six miles.
Facilities: Outhouses, hiking, nature trails.

Stewart Park

Located near the village of Mt. Horeb, this park features seven-acre Stewart Lake. The artificial lake sits on a spring-fed tributary of Blue Mounds Creek and offers opportunities for bass and trout fishing. The park is popular for summer picnicking and cross-country skiing in the winter months.

Directions: Take Highway 18-151 to Mt. Horeb. Turn right on County JG.
Facilities: Picnic tables, picnic shelter, outhouses, toilets, hiking, nature trails, cross-country skiing, playground, boat landing.

Token Creek Park

Token Creek Park offers a wide variety of recreational facilities, including five large-group shelters, volleyball courts, bridle trails, 38 campsites and a separate group camping area. An elevated boardwalk meanders through a sedge meadow marsh, providing an opportunity to view wildlife and unique vegetation. Winter recreation includes a cross-country ski trail and access to an extensive network of snowmobile trails. Many of the park's facilities are handicapped accessible.

Directions: Park entrance is on Highway 51 north of Madison.
Facilities: Picnic tables, picnic shelters, toilets, tent sites, trailer sites, hiking, nature trails, cross-country skiing, volleyball, playground.

Viking Park

Located on the Yahara River just north of Stoughton, Viking Park offers a nature trail, a canoe launch and lagoons for shoreline fishing.

Directions: From Madison, go south on Highway 51 to County B. Take County B east to County N, where the park is located.

Facilities: Picnic tables, picnic shelter, outhouses, hiking, nature trail, boat landing.

Walking Iron Park

Walking Iron Park is undeveloped, but the northern portion contains a native sand prairie and a nature trail along Marsh Creek.

Directions: Take Highway 14 to County Y and go north. Turn west on Hudson Road.

Facilities: Picnic tables, nature trails.

Yahara Heights/Cherokee Marsh

Cherokee Marsh is the largest remaining wetland in Dane County, and Yahara Heights Park fronts more than 3,000 feet of the Yahara River basin. Together, the area provides habitat for birds, wildlife, aquatic life and wetland vegetation, which visitors can view first-hand on the park's nature trails.

Directions: Go north from Madison on Highway 113 to its intersection with County M. The entrance is on the west side of Highway 113.

Facilities: Hiking, nature trails.

DODGE COUNTY

Contact: Dodge County Planning and Development
Dodge County Administration Building
127 East Oak St.
Juneau, WI 53029-1329
(414) 386-3705

Astico Park

The historic Danville Mill Pond surrounds all three sides of this wooded peninsula on the Crawfish River. An expansive river shoreline offers opportunities for canoeing and fishing. Forty-five campsites (25 with electricity), showers and firewood are available to campers. Bring jugs to collect fresh water from the park's two artesian wells.

Directions: Take Highway 60 three miles east of Columbus to County TT.
Facilities: Picnic tables, picnic shelters, outhouses, toilets, tent sites, trailer sites, hiking, playground, canoe landing.

Derge Park

Located on the west-central shore of 6,500-acre Beaver Dam Lake, Derge Park is a popular spot for large group gatherings. Facilities include an enclosed shelter building, grills, 25 campsites with electricity and a boat launch. Hickory trees provide ample shade throughout the park.
Directions: Take Highway 151 to County G, and County G to County CP.
Facilities: Picnic tables, picnic shelters, outhouses, tent sites, trailer sites, playground, boat landing.

Horicon Ledge Park

The natural rock ledge of the Niagara Escarpment divides Horicon Ledge Park into upper and lower areas, providing an overlook of the Horicon Marsh. Wooded with pines, the upper portion offers 45 campsites, hiking trails that wind along the ledge, and picnic and play areas. Group campsites are also available.
Directions: From Beaver Dam, take Highway 33 east to County TW. Go north on County TW to Raaschs Hill Road and turn east. Go ¾ mile and turn north on Park Road.
Facilities: Picnic tables, picnic shelters, outhouses, tent sites, hiking, playground.

DOOR COUNTY

Contact: County of Door
Airport and Parks
3418 Park Drive
Sturgeon Bay, WI 54235
(414) 743-3636

Baileys Harbor Ridges Park

Most noted for its two lighthouses used as navigational aids in bygone days, Baileys Harbor Ridges Park offers 400 feet of sand beach for swimming and sunning. Hike along the series of ridges for a glimpse of some of the rarest wildflowers in Wisconsin.
Directions: Take Highway 57 to the north side of Baileys Harbor. Go east on Ridges Road ½ mile to the park.
Facilities: Toilets, swimming, beach, hiking.

Cave Point Park

Underwater caves, limestone cliffs and the view of Lake Michigan make this park a popular destination. Visitors will have opportunities to fish, scuba dive, hike along the wave-worn bluffs, or relax in the picnic area.

Directions: Take Highway 57 north one mile from Valmy to County WD. Go east on County WD to the end of the road. The park is inside Whitefish Dunes State Park.

Facilities: Picnic tables, outhouses, hiking.

Chaudoir's Dock Park

This small park provides boat access to Green Bay and a large fishing dock. Local residents often picnic here.

Directions: Take Highway 57 west of Brussels to County N. Go west on County N to the end of the road.

Facilities: Picnic tables, outhouses, boat landing.

Door Bluff Headlands Sanctuary

Situated at the most northern point of the Door Peninsula, this sanctuary is undeveloped and being preserved in its natural state. Its vertical headlands rise up from the waters of Green Bay, one of the few such formations in the country.

Directions: Take Highway 42 to downtown Ellison Bay. Go north on Garret Bay Road, west on Door Bluff Road, and then turn right on Door Bluff Park Road, which dead-ends at the park.

Facilities: Hiking.

Door County Fair Park

This Sturgeon Bay park is used for a variety of special events, including horse shows, 4-H events and the Saturday flea market held during the months of June, July and August.

Directions: Take Highway 42-57 into Sturgeon Bay to Michigan Street. Go west on Michigan Street to 14th Avenue and drive north.

Facilities: Toilets.

Ellison Bluff Park

A trail along the park's 100-foot bluff offers scenic overlooks of Green Bay and Ellison Bay. Visitors can enjoy a picnic here in wooded, quiet isolation.

Directions: Go one mile south of Ellison Bay on Highway 42 to Porcupine Bay Road. Go west to Grasse Lane and turn right. The road dead-ends at the park.

Facilities: Picnic tables, outhouses, hiking.

Forestville Dam Park

Small fishing boats and canoes can access the Forestville Pond, once used to power a 19th-century grist mill. Visitors can swim and sun on the sand beach or watch for the wild waterfowl that frequent the pond.

Directions: Take Highway 42 to Forestville. Go west on County J to Mill Road and turn right.

Facilities: Picnic tables, swimming, beach, boat landing.

Frank E. Murphy Park

Located on the Green Bay shore in the town of Egg Harbor, Frank E. Murphy Park offers opportunities to swim and sun from its 1,600 feet of sand beach. Other facilities include a large fishing dock, boat launch, volleyball court and seven acres of woodland.

Directions: Take Highway 42 two miles north of Carlsville. Go north on County G to the park, located at the intersection of County G and County B.

Facilities: Picnic tables, outhouses, swimming, beach, volleyball, playground, boat landing.

Lily Bay Park

Boat landing on Lily Bay.

Directions: Take Highway 42-57 to Sturgeon Bay. Go east on County T four miles to its intersection with Glidden Drive.

Facilities: Boat landing only.

Lyle-Harter-Matter Sanctuary

Two marshy lakes in this designated sanctuary serve as nesting grounds for several species of waterfowl. A 50-foot sand dune sits in the northeastern corner of the park.

Directions: Take Highway 57 2½ miles north of Jacksonport. Enter through Meridian Park.

Facilities: None.

Meridian Park

This heavily wooded 92-acre park is undeveloped except for a wayside on Highway 57 between Jacksonport and Baileys Harbor, where travelers can stop for a picnic. A series of sand ridges near the highway graduate into major sand-dune forms in the northwest corner of the park.

Directions: Take Highway 57 2½ miles north of Jacksonport to the park entrance.

Facilities: Picnic tables, outhouses.

Percy Johnson Memorial Park

Tall pines shelter a picnic area in the northeast corner of this five-acre park on Washington Island. The eastern side offers a sand beach for swimming and sunning on Lake Michigan.

Directions: From the car ferry on Washington Island, take Lakeview Road to its intersection with Shellswick Drive on the east side of the island.

Facilities: Picnic tables, outhouses, swimming, beach, playground.

Quarry Park

This newly developed park on Sturgeon Bay offers dock fishing, boat access to the bay and picnic facilities.

Directions: Take Highway 42-57 north of Sturgeon Bay to County BB. Go west on County BB to County B (Bayshore Drive). Go north on County B three miles to the park.

Facilities: Picnic tables, outhouses, playground, boat landing.

Robert LaSalle Park

This park's three-tiered landscape, connected by stairs, provides opportunities for a wide range of outdoor activity. The pebble beach lines Lake Michigan, a grassy upland area offers a baseball and game field and, still higher, a wooded area offers a picnic area and a scenic lake view. It is said to be the spot where French explorer Robert LaSalle landed in 1679.

Directions: Take Highway 42 to Forestville. Go east on County J to County U. Go south ½ mile on County U to the park's upper level entrance. Go north ½ mile on County U to the park's lower level entrance.

Facilities: Picnic tables, outhouses, swimming, beach, baseball, volleyball.

Sugar Creek Park

Popular with smelt-dippers, Sugar Creek runs through this largely undeveloped park. Visitors will find a few picnic spots in addition to the fair-weather boat landing.

Directions: Take Highway 57 to County N. Go north three miles on County N.

Facilities: Picnic tables, outhouses, boat landing.

Tornado Memorial Park

This wayside picnic site, which became the first county park in 1927, serves as a memorial to the former village of Williamsonville, destroyed by fire in 1871.

Directions: Take Highway 57 four miles northeast of Brussels to its intersection with County K.

Facilities: Picnic tables, outhouses.

DOUGLAS COUNTY

Contact: Douglas County Forestry Department
Box 211
Solon Springs, WI 54873
(715) 378-2219

Anna-Gene Park

Adjacent to Lyman Lake, this park provides a nice spot for a picnic. There is also a boat landing and a playground.

Directions: From Solon Springs, take Highway 53 north seven miles to County L. Turn west and travel 7½ miles to E. Lyman Lake Road. Turn west and continue ¾ mile to the park.

Facilities: Picnic tables, outhouses, playground, boat landing.

Bass Lake Park

A day-use park, Bass Lake is mainly a swimming spot. The park also offers picnic tables.

Directions: From Solon Springs, take County A northeast seven miles to Muskrat Lake Road. Turn south and go 2½ miles to Bass Lake Road. Go south ½ mile to the park.

Facilities: Picnic tables, outhouses, swimming.

Douglas County Wildlife Area

Commonly known as "The Bird Sanctuary," the Douglas County Wildlife Area is designated a fish and wildlife management area. The sanctuary maintains a plant and animal type called the pine barrens, once common in northwestern Wisconsin. Blueberries can be picked throughout the park; you may want to enjoy them at the picnic tables provided throughout the park.

Directions: From Highway 53 south of Solon Springs, take County M west ½ mile to Bird Road. Turn north and continue ½ mile to the park.

Facilities: Picnic tables, hiking, cross-country skiing.

Gordon Dam Park

Located at the St. Croix Flowage Dam, this park is a popular fishing spot, where anglers can expect to catch muskellunge, northern pike, bass, walleye, pan fish, bullheads and an occasional sturgeon. Anglers can fish from a 24-foot handicapped-accessible lighted dock, or launch a boat and join the many canoeists exploring the flowage's meandering shoreline and scattered islands. After the catch, a handicapped-accessible fish-cleaning house is available, along with a number of picnic areas complete with tables, grills and fire rings. Visitors can also spend the night camping in one of the 33 campsites, 12 of which have electricity.

Directions: From Highway 53 in Gordon, take County Y west seven miles to the park.

Facilities: Picnic tables, outhouses, tent sites, trailer sites, swimming, cross-country skiing, boat landing.

Lake Minnesuing Park

Swimmers appreciate this park for its direct access to Minnesuing Lake. The park also provides picnic tables for visitor use.

Directions: From Highway 53, take County B east four miles to County P. Turn south and continue 2½ miles to the park.

Facilities: Picnic tables, outhouses, swimming.

Lucius Woods Park

Located on the 855-acre Upper St. Croix Lake, Lucius Woods County Park offers a large handicapped-accessible sand beach, along with dressing rooms, picnic areas and a playground. The park is very popular for fishing, boating and waterskiing. Several public boat landings are near the park. Visitors can walk along Park Creek on a self-guided nature trail. An open performing arts center is also located in the park and often features concerts by the Duluth-Superior Symphony Orchestra. There are 24 campsites, 11 with electricity.

Directions: The park is located in Solon Springs, directly off Highway 53 on Marion Avenue.

Facilities: Picnic tables, picnic shelter, outhouses, toilets, tent sites, trailer sites, swimming, beach, dressing rooms, hiking, playground.

Mooney Dam Park

This park is developed primarily for camping use, with 13 campsites on the Eau Claire River. A boat landing is also located in the park.

Directions: From Gordon, go 10 miles east on County Y to S. Mail Road. Turn south and travel ¼ mile to the park.

Facilities: Outhouses, tent sites, trailer sites, boat landing.

DUNN COUNTY

Contact: Dunn County Parks
800 Wilson Ave.
Menomonie, WI 54751
(715) 232-1651

Allen Champney Memorial Park

This boat landing and picnic area on Tainter Lake receives mostly local use. Anglers will find muskie, northern pike, walleye, large and smallmouth bass, and assorted pan fish.

Directions: Take Highway 94 to County B. Go north on County B to Lake Road, and north on Lake Road to Champney Road.

Facilities: Picnic tables, picnic shelter, outhouses, playground, boat landing.

Caddie Woodlawn Historical Park

The original 1856 lumber house of former resident Caddie Woodlawn still stands here. The park also has picnic and playground facilities.

Directions: Take Highway 25 south of Downsville. The park is on the east side of the highway.

Facilities: Picnic tables, picnic shelter, outhouses, playground.

Eau Galle Dam Park

This small park on Lake Eau Galle is well-kept, but is limited to a few picnic tables and grills.

Directions: Take Highway 25 to County Y and go west. Go south at County Z. The park is located in the town of Eau Galle.

Facilities: Picnic tables, outhouses.

Eau Galle Sportsman's Landing

Boat landing on Lake Eau Galle.

Directions: Take Highway 25 to County Y and go west. Go south at County Z. The park is located in the town of Eau Galle.

Facilities: Outhouses, boat landing.

Lamb's Creek Park

This site provides access to Lamb's Creek, a deep channel of the Red Cedar River, where anglers will find pan fish, walleye and northern pike. The park's picnic facilities, which include grills, are used primarily by local residents.

Directions: Take Highway 94 to County B and go north. Go west on County BB to County G.

Facilities: Picnic tables, picnic shelter, outhouses, playground, boat landing.

Menomin Park

This large rustic park on Lake Menomin offers opportunities to hike and fish, though the lake usually turns very green by summer. The park's wild state, except for a small picnic area, allows for frequent deer and eagle sightings.

Directions: Take Highway 12-29 east of Menomonie to County MMM. Go north on County MMM to Red Cedar Road and go west.
Facilities: Picnic tables, picnic shelter, hiking.

Myron Park

Campers who enjoy "roughing it" will appreciate Myron Park, located on the Red Cedar River. In addition to its 50 campsites, hiking, fishing and boating opportunities, the park offers visitors a chance to stroll through its museum of antique farm machinery.

Directions: Take Highway 64 to County M. Go north on County M to County I.
Facilities: Picnic tables, picnic shelter, outhouses, tent sites, trailer sites, hiking, playground, boat landing.

Northwest Landing

This site is used mostly as a boat access to Tainter Lake, noted for its ample supply of muskellunge, walleye, northern pike, large and smallmouth bass and pan fish. The boat dock is handicapped accessible and the picnic area contains grills.

Directions: Take Highway 25 to County D and go east. Go south at Elk Point Road, and west on Twin Bay Road.
Facilities: Picnic tables, picnic shelter, outhouses, boat landing.

Peninsula Park

Boat landing on Tainter Lake.

Directions: Take Highway 170 to County D. Go south on County D to Peninsula Road.
Facilities: Boat landing only.

Pineview Park

Pineview's location on Lake Eau Galle makes it a popular spot for fishing (pan fish abound), picnicking and swimming. The boat dock and fishing pier are handicapped accessible, and the picnic area is equipped with grills.

Directions: Take Highway 25 to County Y and go west. Go north at County Z to Pine Point Lane. Turn west. The park is located in the town of Eau Galle.
Facilities: Picnic tables, picnic shelter, outhouses, swimming, beach, dressing rooms, boat landing.

Recreation Park

Recreation Park offers a variety of activities year-round. During the summer months, it is commonly used for horse shows, stock-car racing, wedding receptions and family gatherings. An outdoor ice-skating rink is open from mid-October to March. Group campsites are available by reservation.

Directions: From Highway 94, go south on County B to Highway 12-29. Take Highway 12-29 west to 17th Street in Menomonie.

Facilities: Picnic tables, picnic shelters, toilets, playground.

Rock Falls Park

A tiny gazebo shelters picnickers in this small but well-kept park in Rock Falls.

Directions: Take Highway 85 to Rock Falls. The park is located on the north side of the highway.

Facilities: Picnic tables, picnic shelter.

Thatcher Park

Anglers will appreciate the small trout stream, the south fork of the Hay River, that winds through this 1.5-acre park. A few picnic tables and grills are available.

Directions: Take Highway 64 to County K and go north.

Facilities: Picnic tables, outhouses.

22-Mile Ford Wayside

This two-acre wayside on the Red Cedar River offers picnic facilities, including grills, and a boat launch. Unfortunately, the park is often vandalized.

Directions: Take Highway 40 to Colfax. Go north on County M.

Facilities: Picnic tables, picnic shelter, outhouses, playground, boat landing.

Zielie Park

Located on Elk Creek, Zielie Park is used almost exclusively as a trout-fishing spot. Two picnic tables are provided.

Directions: From Menomonie, take Highway 12-29 east to County E. Go west on County E.

Facilities: Picnic tables.

EAU CLAIRE COUNTY

Contact: Eau Claire County
Parks and Forest Department
227 1st Street West
Altoona, WI 54720
(715) 839-4738

Beaver Creek Reserve

The Beaver Creek Reserve is a 360-acre environmental and outdoor recreation center, which encompasses a youth camp, the Wise Nature Center and Hobbs Observatory. Visitors can hike, snowshoe, or ski the nature trails, and test their agility on the obstacle course. One nature trail is handicapped accessible. During the summer months, the Hobbs Observatory is open for stargazing on clear Saturday evenings.

Directions: From Fall Creek, go north on County K about four miles to the reserve.

Facilities: Toilets, hiking, nature trails, cross-country skiing.

Big Falls Park

Picnickers and sunbathers will appreciate the wild surroundings here, where the Eau Claire River washes over huge granite rock outcroppings. Kick off your shoes to wade in the river, launch a canoe, or fish from the boulder-lined shores.

Directions: From Eau Claire, take Highway 53 to County Q (Birch Street). Go east nine miles on County Q, and turn right onto County UN. The park entrance is ½ mile down this road.

Facilities: Picnic tables, outhouses, canoe landing.

Coon Fork Park

Located on 80-acre Coon Fork Lake, 30 miles east of Eau Claire, Coon Fork Park offers 88 wooded campsites, swimming beaches and canoe, paddleboat and rowboat rentals. On the west side of the lake, in the day-use area, visitors will find a nature trail for hiking and cross-country skiing in the winter, picnic areas, basketball and volleyball courts, more swimming beaches and various boat landings. Anglers can fish Coon Fork Lake for its muskellunge, bass, crappie and pan fish.

Directions: To get to the day-use area of the park, take Highway 12 east from Augusta to County CF. The entrance is on the right side of the road. To get to the camping area, continue along County CF across Coon Creek to the entrance.

Facilities: Picnic tables, picnic shelter, outhouses, toilets, tent sites, trailer sites, swimming, beach, dressing rooms, hiking, nature trails, cross-country skiing, volleyball, playground, boat landing.

Harstad Park

Overlooking the Eau Claire River, Harstad Park offers scenic picnic facilities for large group gatherings, a playground and access for canoeing and fishing. Nature-lovers will like the seclusion and ruggedness of the park's 27 wooded campsites.

Rent a canoe or paddleboat at Coon Fork Park in Eau Claire County.

Directions: Take Highway 12 north from Augusta to County HH. Go north on County HH to County HHH. The park entrance is off this road.
Facilities: Picnic tables, picnic shelter, outhouses, tent sites, trailer sites, baseball, playground, canoe landing.

Lake Altoona Park

The large sand beach on 850-acre Lake Altoona, just a few miles from downtown Eau Claire, provides supervised summertime swimming, sunning and concessions. Other facilities include a boat landing, picnic grills, horseshoe pits and volleyball. Visitors can reserve the clubhouse.
Directions: Take Highway 53 to County A and go east. Turn left at North Wilson and right at Lake Road.
Facilities: Picnic tables, picnic shelter, toilets, swimming, beach, dressing rooms, volleyball, playground, boat landing.

Lake Eau Claire Park

Located on the west shore of 1,118-acre Lake Eau Claire, this park contains a picnic area with grills, volleyball court, horseshoe pits and a playground. Visitors can fish here, but boat access to the lake is down the road at a separate site.

Directions: From Augusta, take Highway 27 north to County SD and go west.
Facilities: Picnic tables, picnic shelter, outhouses, cross-country skiing, baseball, volleyball.

L.L. Phillips Park

A 1.2-mile nature trail meanders through this park's diverse landscape. Visitors can explore pine plantations, stands of aspen, spruce and oak trees, an oxbow lake and the trout-stocked Seven Mile Creek. The park is open for cross-country skiing in the winter.
Directions: Take Highway 53 to County Q (Birch Street) and go east. Take County Q to County QQ and turn right. The park entrance is about 4½ miles down the road.
Facilities: Picnic tables, picnic shelter, outhouses, hiking, nature trails, cross-country skiing.

Lowes Creek Park

Located along the shores of Lowes Creek, Lowes Creek Park offers a fitness and mountain bike trail and cross-country ski trails. Lowes Creek is known for its excellent supply of trout.
Directions: Take Highway 93 south from Eau Claire to County S (Golf Road) and turn right. Turn left at South Lowes Creek Road and go about 1½ miles to the park entrance.
Facilities: Picnic tables, picnic shelter, outhouses, cross-country skiing.

FLORENCE COUNTY

Contact: Florence Natural Resource Center
HC1, Box 83
Florence, WI 54121
(715) 528-5377

Emily Lake Park

Located on 191-acre Emily Lake south of Florence, this park offers 18 campsites, a swimming beach and picnic facilities. Anglers can fish from a boat or the fishing pier for northern pike, walleye, largemouth bass and pan fish.
Directions: From Florence, take Highway 101 south to County D. Go east on County D to the park.
Facilities: Picnic tables, picnic shelter, outhouses, tent sites, trailer sites, swimming, beach, dressing rooms, playground, boat landing.

Fisher Lake Park

Fisher Lake's 54 acres host populations of northern pike, bass, pan fish and trout. Visitors can picnic, play baseball, launch a boat, or relax on the sand beach.

Directions: From Florence, go ½ mile south on County NN to the park.

Facilities: Picnic tables, outhouses, swimming, beach, dressing rooms, baseball, boat landing.

Florence County Fairgrounds

This facility is used for local exhibitions and the county fair. Visitors can enjoy a picnic or a game of baseball or soccer.

Directions: From Florence, go south on County N.

Facilities: Picnic tables, picnic shelter, outhouses, baseball.

Kenneth Thompson Memorial Park

This remote, quiet park serves as a habitat for loons and nesting osprey. Visitors can launch a boat to fish 55-acre Siedel Lake for northern pike, bass and pan fish.

Directions: Take Highway 101 south from Florence to the lake access road on the north side of the highway, near where Siedel Lake Creek crosses the road.

Facilities: Picnic tables, boat landing.

Keyes Lake Park

Keyes Lake's crystal-clear waters make for good swimming and fishing for northern pike, walleye, pan fish and bass. The park has picnic facilities, volleyball courts, a beach and a boat landing. The boat dock, swimming area and restrooms are handicapped accessible.

Directions: Take Highway 101 three miles south of Florence.

Facilities: Picnic tables, picnic shelter, outhouses, swimming, beach, dressing room, volleyball, boat landing.

Loon Lake Park

Walk-in access to 53-acre Loon Lake, where anglers will find northern pike, largemouth bass and pan fish.

Directions: Take Highway 101 south of Highway 70. The park is on the west side of the highway.

Facilities: None.

Popple River Park

The Popple River is an undeveloped, scenic, designated "wild" river, good for canoeing and kayaking. The park offers canoe and kayak access, picnic tables and a spot to fish for brook, brown and rainbow trout.

Directions: Go 12 miles south of Florence on Highway 101.
Facilities: Picnic tables, canoe landing.

Vagabond Park

Located on 928-acre Twin Falls Flowage, Vagabond Park has a sand beach, picnic area and a boat landing. The flowage is scenic and semiprimitive, with islands and very few homes. Anglers will find northern pike, walleye, bass and pan fish. A ski team performs at the park twice a week.

    Directions: Take Highway 2 nine miles east of Florence.
    Facilities: Picnic tables, outhouses, swimming, beach, boat landing.

In winter, hiking paths become cross-country skiing trails at county parks throughout the state.

West Bass Lake Park

The oak forest in West Bass Lake Park offers a secluded, quiet spot to camp. Fifteen campsites are available, plus opportunities to swim, sun on the beach, picnic, and take a boat out on West Bass Lake. The 57-acre lake has largemouth bass and pan fish.

Directions: Take Highway 101 to County C. Go east on County C.

Facilities: Picnic tables, outhouses, tent sites, trailer sites, swimming, beach, dressing rooms, playground, boat landing.

FOND DU LAC COUNTY

Contact: Fond du Lac County Planning/
Parks Department
City-County Government Center
160 South Macy St.
Fond du Lac, WI 54935
(414) 929-3135

Columbia Park

An 80-foot observation tower at Columbia Park overlooks Lake Winnebago, a favorite of boating and fishing enthusiasts. Located on the east shore of the lake, the park offers 40 open-field campsites, boat slip rentals and a picnic area.

Directions: Take Highway 151 about 10 miles north of Fond du Lac to County W. Go west on County W.

Facilities: Picnic tables, picnic shelter, outhouses, toilets, tent sites, trailer sites, playground, boat landing.

Fond du Lac County Fairgrounds

Used for a range of special events and activities year-round, the Fond du Lac County Fairgrounds offers a swimming pool, baseball diamond, playground equipment and an indoor ice-skating rink.

Directions: Take Highway 41 to Highway 175 (Main Street). Go north on Highway 175 to Pioneer Road. Take Pioneer Road east to Martin Avenue and go north to the park entrance.

Facilities: Toilets, swimming, baseball, playground.

Highway 45 Wayside

This park is used primarily as an access to Lake Winnebago. The boat launch is suitable for canoes and cartop boats, and, in the winter months, the wayside offers a spot to ice fish.

Directions: Take Highway 45 three miles north of Fond du Lac. The wayside is located on the east side of the highway.
Facilities: Picnic tables, picnic shelter, toilets, boat landing.

Hobbs Woods

Two and a half miles of interpretive nature trails wind through 60-acre Hobbs Woods, which visitors can hike in the warm months and cross-country ski in the winter. A trout stream, Parson's Creek, flows through the park.
   Directions: Take Highway 175 south of Fond du Lac to County B. Go west on County B to South Hickory Road and go south.
   Facilities: Hiking, nature trails, cross-country skiing.

Northwoods Park

Thirty-five acres of undeveloped woodland in Northwoods County Park provide opportunities for hiking, cross-country skiing and picnics in the midst of undisturbed nature.
   Directions: Take Highway 26 north about four miles from the village of Rosendale. The park is located on the east side of the highway.
   Facilities: Picnic tables, hiking, nature trails, cross-country skiing.

Roosevelt Park

Roosevelt Park offers 900 feet of Lake Winnebago shoreline for swimming, sunning, and playing on the beach. Picnic tables are provided.
   Directions: Take Highway 41 in Fond du Lac to Highway 175. Go north on Highway 175 to Highway 151. Go east two miles on Highway 151 to the park entrance.
   Facilities: Picnic tables, toilets, swimming, beach.

Waupun Park

Red oak, hard maple, white ash and white oak trees populate the northeastern 40 acres of Fond du Lac's largest county park, where a nature trail winds through a scientific area. Forty-two campsites, with electricity, and showers are available. The park also offers a swimming pool, baseball field, playground and picnic area.
   Directions: Take Highway 151 to Highway 49 at Waupun. Go west on Highway 49 to County MMM and go north. County MMM runs through the park.
   Facilities: Picnic tables, picnic shelter, outhouses, tent sites, trailer sites, swimming, hiking, cross-country skiing, baseball, playground.

Wolf Lake Park

Wolf Lake County Park is divided into two separate units, both situated on Wolf Lake. The southern portion offers boat access to the lake; the northern portion has a swimming beach, picnic area and playground. Wolf Lake is small but heavily used for swimming, boating, waterskiing, and fishing.

Directions: Take Highway 149 into the town of Marshfield, about 12 miles northeast of Fond du Lac. The park is located along the highway.

Facilities: Picnic tables, outhouses, swimming, beach, dressing rooms, playground, boat landing.

FOREST COUNTY

Contact: Forest County Forestry Department
Courthouse
200 East Madison
Crandon, WI 54520
(715) 478-3475

Veteran's Memorial Park

Located just south of Crandon on Lake Metonga, Veteran's Memorial Park offers 65 campsites, some with electricity, along 900 feet of sandy beach. The lake water is clear and shallow for at least 100 feet from shore, making it ideal for family swimming. Anglers will find an abundance of fish, including walleye, northern pike, large and smallmouth bass, bluegill, black crappie, rock bass, pumpkinseed and white sucker. Handicapped-accessible facilities are available.

Directions: From Crandon, take Highway 55 to County W. Go south on County W to Keith Siding Road and go west. Turn right (north) on East Shore Road, where the park is located.

Facilities: Picnic tables, picnic shelter, outhouses, tent sites, trailer sites, swimming, beach, volleyball, playground, boat landing.

GRANT COUNTY

Contact: Grant County Extension Office
Box 31
Lancaster, WI 53813
(608) 723-2125

Banfield Bridge Recreation Area

A boat landing in the park provides direct access to the Mississippi River. There is also a picnic table for visitor use.

Directions: From Dickeyville, travel west on Highway 61 to Indian Creek Road. Turn left and travel three miles to the access.
Facilities: Picnic table, boat landing.

Blue River Recreation Area

Located on the Wisconsin River, this park provides a boat landing, picnic table and grill for visitor use.
Directions: From Blue River, take County T north. The park is just south of the Wisconsin River bridge.
Facilities: Picnic table, outhouses, boat landing.

Boscobel Recreation Area

A boat landing on the Wisconsin River allows anglers a chance to hook northern pike, smallmouth bass, walleye, sauger, sturgeon, bluegill, eel and catfish. Boscobel Recreation Area also has a picnic area with picnic tables, shelter and grills.
Directions: From Boscobel, take Highway 61 north. The park is just south of the Wisconsin River bridge.
Facilities: Picnic tables, picnic shelter, outhouses, boat landing.

Glen Haven Recreation Area

This park offers access to the Mississippi River from a boat landing in the park. Picnic tables and a grill are also available.
Directions: In the town of Glen Haven, go north on the main street to the river.
Facilities: Picnic tables, outhouses, boat landing.

McCartney Recreation Area

While providing access to the Mississippi River from a boat landing, the park also has picnic tables and a grill.
Directions: Halfway between Cassville and Potosi on Highway 133, turn west on County N. Continue for two miles to the landing.
Facilities: Picnic tables, outhouses, boat landing.

Millville Recreation Area

The boat landing in this park provides access to the Wisconsin River. The park also contains picnic tables and a grill.
Directions: From Boscobel, take Highway 133 west to County C. Turn west on C and travel just past the town of Millville to the junction with Barker Hollow Road.
Facilities: Picnic tables, outhouses, boat landing.

O'Leary's Lake Recreation Area

This park has two boat landings on the Mississippi River.
Directions: From Platteville, take Highway 151 southwest past Dickeyville to Eagle Point Road. Turn west and continue to the landing.
Facilities: Outhouses, boat landings.

Potosi-Tennyson Recreation Area

This small, rustic park offers a boat landing for access onto the Mississippi River.
Directions: From Highway 61 north of Tennyson, take Highway 133 west 2½ miles to the landing.
Facilities: Boat landing only.

Woodman Recreation Area

This park provides a boat landing on the Wisconsin River, picnic table and grill.
Directions: From Boscobel, take Highway 133 west 2½ miles past the town of Woodman.
Facilities: Picnic table, outhouses, boat landing.

Wyalusing Recreation Area

A sand beach at this park allows visitors to swim in the Mississippi River. Anglers also appreciate the access to the river, where they can hook pan fish, large and smallmouth bass, walleye, northern pike, sauger and catfish. A boat landing is provided. Picnic areas are spread throughout the park, offering a shelter, numerous picnic tables and several grills.
Directions: The park is located directly in the town of Wyalusing on County X.
Facilities: Picnic tables, picnic shelter, outhouses, swimming, beach, boat landing.

GREEN COUNTY

Contact: Green County Clerk's Office
1016 16th Ave.
Monroe, WI 53566
(608) 328-9430

Clarence Bridge Park

Clarence Bridge Park is located on the Sugar River, noted for its ample supply of catfish. The park provides a boat launch and picnic facilities.

Directions: Take Highway 11-81 to its intersection with Mt. Hope Road, about one mile west of Brodhead, where the park is located.
Facilities: Picnic tables, outhouses, boat landing.

Pleasant View Park

This wooded park offers a nature trail for hiking, a picnic area and playground.
Directions: From Monroe, take Highway 81 northwest about one mile to its intersection with County N.
Facilities: Picnic shelter, picnic tables, toilets, hiking, nature trail, playground.

GREEN LAKE COUNTY

Contact: Green Lake County Clerk's Office
P.O. Box 3188
Green Lake, WI 54941
(414) 294-4005

Big Twin Park

Located on 78-acre Big Twin Lake, this small park offers a grassy picnic area, a grill and a boat launch. Anglers will find northern pike, walleye and large-mouth bass.
Directions: Take Highway 73 to its intersection with County K. Go east on County K about 3½ miles to the park entrance.
Facilities: Picnic tables, outhouses.

Dodge Memorial Park

Dodge Memorial Park provides access to Green Lake, Wisconsin's deepest lake, noted for its supply of trout. Totaling more than 7,000 acres, Green Lake is popular with boaters, water-skiers, anglers and beach-goers. This large park offers picnic areas with grills, volleyball, a swimming beach and a snack bar.
Directions: Take Highway 73 to its intersection with County K. Go east on County K one mile to the park entrance.
Facilities: Picnic tables, picnic shelter, toilets, swimming, beach, volleyball, boat landing.

Kingston-Spring Lake Park

Anglers will appreciate the northern pike, walleye, and particularly the pan fish in this 70-acre, deep spring lake. Visitors will find picnic tables, grills and a 300-foot sand swimming beach.

Directions: Take Highway 44 west of Highway 73 to County FF. The park is located on County FF about one mile southwest of Kingston.

Facilities: Picnic tables, outhouses, swimming, beach, boat landing.

Lake Maria Park

Stop for a picnic or cast a line for pan fish in this small park on 596-acre Lake Maria, located just south of Markesan. The park also provides a boat launch, picnic tables and a grill.

Directions: Take Highway 73 about three miles south of Markesan. The park access road is signed on Highway 73.

Facilities: Picnic tables, outhouses, boat landing.

Spring Valley Park

Boat landing on Green Lake County's *other* Spring Lake (there are two; see Kingston-Spring Lake Park listing). Anglers will find northern pike, walleye and pan fish.

Directions: Take Highway 73 to its intersection with County K. Go west three miles on County K to the park.

Facilities: Outhouses, boat landing.

Sunset Park

Two-acre Sunset Park provides access for boating, fishing and waterskiing on Green Lake. The lake spans more than 7,000 acres and, though most noted for its supply of trout, also has populations of northern pike and walleye. Picnic tables and grills are provided.

Directions: Take Highway 23 to County A. The park is located one mile southeast of the city of Green Lake on County A.

Facilities: Picnic tables, outhouses, boat landing.

Zobel Memorial Park

This 40-acre wayside offers a panoramic view of the area from its overlook tower. The picnic area is equipped with tables and grills.

Directions: Take Highway 49 one mile north of the city of Green Lake.

Facilities: Picnic tables, picnic shelter, outhouses.

IOWA COUNTY

Contact: Blackhawk Lake Recreation Area
2025 County BH
Highland, WI 53543
(608) 623-2707

Blackhawk Lake Recreation Area

Surrounded by public hunting grounds, Blackhawk Lake Recreation Area is densely wooded and traversed by 11 miles of hiking and cross-county ski trails. The park offers 123 open-field and wooded campsites, 12 group campsites, electricity and showers. Water enthusiasts will appreciate 220-acre Blackhawk Lake, where they can boat, sail, wind surf, scuba dive, swim, and fish. A camp store rents canoes, boats and pontoons in the summer. Other recreation opportunities include sand volleyball, horseshoes, bird watching, picnicking, a nature center and naturalist-led talks and hikes.

Directions: Take Highway 80 south from Highland to County BH. Go east on County BH to the park entrance.

Facilities: Picnic tables, picnic shelters, toilets, tent sites, trailer sites, swimming, beach, dressing rooms, hiking, nature trails, cross-country skiing, volleyball, playground, boat landing.

IRON COUNTY

Contact: Iron County Parks Department
300 Taconite
Hurley, WI 54534
(715) 561-2697

Gile Park

Located on the northern shore of the Gile Flowage, Gile Park offers several boat landings, a swimming area and picnic facilities with fireplaces. Primitive camping is allowed on all the islands in the flowage, assuming you have a boat to get there. Anglers will find muskellunge, bass, walleye and northern pike.

Directions: Take Highway 77 into Gile, west of Hurley, where the park is located.

Facilities: Picnic tables, picnic shelter, toilets, tent sites, trailer sites, swimming, dressing rooms, playground, boat landing.

Lake of the Falls Park

Lake of the Falls Park encompasses 40 acres and a small waterfall on the 19,000-acre Turtle Flambeau Flowage, where visitors can launch a boat and fish for muskellunge, bass, walleye and northern pike. The park offers 30 open-field campsites, a swimming area and a picnic area equipped with fireplaces.

Directions: Take Highway 51 to County FF and go southwest. Follow County FF to the park.

Facilities: Picnic tables, picnic shelter, outhouses, tent sites, trailer sites, playground, boat landing.

Potato River Falls Recreation Area

After a long hike through the woods down to the river, visitors can view the 90-foot drop of Potato River Falls. Campers seeking primitive conditions can also pitch a tent in the park.

Directions: From Hurley, take Highway 2 west to Highway 169 in Cedar. Turn south on 169 and travel 2½ miles to Potato River Falls Road. Turn west and continue two miles.

Facilities: Tent sites, hiking.

Saxon Harbor Park

With 52 boat slips on Lake Superior, this park is much like a marina. The extras include a swimming beach, seven open-field campsites with electricity, a playground and a picnic area with fireplaces.

Directions: Take Highway 2 to Highway 122. Go north on Highway 122 to the park.

Facilities: Picnic tables, picnic shelter, outhouses, tent sites, trailer sites, swimming, dressing rooms, playground, boat landing.

Weber Lake Park

This 10-acre park sits on the shores of tiny but popular Weber Lake, used for summertime swimming and trout-fishing. Seven campsites with electricity are available.

Directions: Take Highway 77 west of Hurley to County E. Go west on County E to the park.

Facilities: Picnic tables, picnic shelter, outhouses, tent sites, trailer sites, swimming, dressing rooms, playground, boat landing.

JACKSON COUNTY

Contact: Jackson County Forestry
and Parks Department
307 Main St.
Black River Falls, WI 54615
(715) 284-0224

East Arbutus Park

The largest and also the busiest of Jackson County's parks, East Arbutus County Park offers 153 campsites and access to electricity and showers. Lake Arbutus is popular with waterskiers, jetskiers, boaters, anglers and beachcombers. Some of the campsites sit lakeside.

Directions: From Black River Falls, take Highway 54 six miles east to County K. Turn north and proceed eight miles to Clay School Road. Turn east and go one mile to the park.

Facilities: Picnic tables, outhouses, tent sites, trailer sites, swimming, beach, hiking, playground, boat landing.

Crawford Hills Park

Primarily an off-road vehicle park, Crawford Hills County Park offers visitors a chance to drive their motorcycles and ATVs along single-track motorcycle trails through the park or to access other county ATV trails. Picnic facilities, a playground and 15 campsites are also available.

Directions: From Black River Falls, take Highway 54 east 15 miles.

Facilities: Picnic tables, picnic shelter, outhouses, tent sites, hiking, playground.

Merlin Lambert Park

Once the site of a logging camp in the 1800s, Merlin Lambert County Park is now a rugged, out-of-the-way park in the Jackson County Forest. Its location on Potter's Flowage attracts anglers in search of pan fish, muskellunge and bass. The park offers 30 campsites, picnic facilities and opportunities to hike a few of the forest's 118,000 acres.

Directions: From Black River Falls, take Highway 54 east 20 miles to McKenna Road. Turn south and continue for four miles.

Facilities: Picnic tables, picnic shelter, outhouses, tent sites, hiking, playground, boat landing.

Spaulding Pond Park

Spaulding Pond is used primarily for summer swimming, though anglers do occasionally find some fish. Picnic tables and six rugged campsites are available.

Directions: From Black River Falls, travel 22 miles east on Highway 54.

Facilities: Picnic tables, outhouses, tent sites, hiking, swimming.

Wazee Lake Recreation Area

The former site of a Jackson County iron mine, Wazee Lake, 355 feet at its maximum depth, now attracts scuba divers. The park also offers a beach, boat landing and fishing opportunities in the lake and on an adjacent pond. Fifteen miles of hiking trail, also used for bicycling, may give visitors a glimpse of two endangered species that inhabit the park: the timber wolf and the Karner blue butterfly. Twelve primitive campsites are available.

Directions: From Black River Falls, take Highway 54 east six miles. Turn south on Brockway Road and continue for four miles.

Facilities: Picnic tables, outhouses, tent sites, trailer sites, swimming, beach, hiking, cross-country skiing, boat landing.

West Arbutus Park

Located on the western shore of Lake Arbutus, this park is heavily used for motorized water recreation, including motor boating, waterskiing and jetskiing. The park also offers 45 campsites, some lakeside, a swimming beach and a picnic area.

Directions: From Black River Falls, take Highway 12 north three miles, then turn east onto County E. Continue into the village of Hatfield to Thunderbird Lane.

Facilities: Picnic tables, outhouses, tent sites, trailer sites, swimming, beach, hiking, playground, boat landing.

JEFFERSON COUNTY

Contact: Jefferson County Parks Department
Courthouse, Room 212
320 S. Main St.
Jefferson, WI 53549
(414) 674-7260

Altpeter Park

Primarily used by neighborhood residents, Altpeter Park contains a playground and baseball backstop. The playground is near the west shore of Lake Koshkonong.

Directions: From Fort Atkinson, take Highway 106 west to North Shore Road. Turn left on North Shore Road to Lamp Road. Travel one block on Lamp Road to the park.

Facilities: Baseball, playground.

Bicentennial Park

Travelers along Highway 26 frequently stop to rest at this 35-acre, largely undeveloped park, where facilities are limited to one picnic table.

Directions: From Jefferson, travel north on Highway 26 to the park, which is about one mile south of Johnson Creek.
Facilities: Picnic table.

Burnt Village Park

Boat landing on the Bark River, primarily used for fishing.
Directions: From Fort Atkinson, take Highway 106 east to County N. Turn south on N and continue to the park, which is two miles north of Cold Spring.
Facilities: Boat landing only.

Busseyville Park

This one-acre park is well-used as a picnic spot by both large and small groups. Recreation facilities include a baseball backstop, basketball court and playground.
Directions: From Fort Atkinson, take Highway 106 west about eight miles to the park.
Facilities: Picnic tables, outhouses, baseball, playground.

Carlin Weld Park

At 78 acres, Carlin Weld is the largest county park in Jefferson County. Picnicking, hiking and fishing the park's small pond are popular warm-weather activities. During the winter months, visitors can cross-country ski and toboggan.
Directions: From Palmyra, take Highway 59 east to County H. Turn north on H and continue to County Z. Turn north on Z and continue ¼ mile to the park.
Facilities: Picnic tables, picnic shelter, outhouses, hiking, cross-country skiing, playground.

Cold Spring Creamery Park

Often used as a rest stop, this small park offers a picnic spot with grills and a shelter.
Directions: From Fort Atkinson, take Highway 59 east to County N. Turn south on N and travel four miles to the park.
Facilities: Picnic tables, picnic shelter, outhouses.

Dahnert Park

The park's baseball diamond and volleyball court are used extensively by organized teams. Located in the small community of Concord, Dahnert/Concord Park also has picnic facilities and a playground.
Directions: From Jefferson, take Highway 18 east to County F. Turn north on F and follow it to Concord Center Drive. The park is located in Concord on Concord Center Drive.
Facilities: Picnic tables, picnic shelter, outhouses, baseball, volleyball, playground.

Indian Mounds and Trail Park

A walking trail takes visitors past 11 Indian effigy mounds and the remains of an ancient Indian walking trail. The park is popular with students and tourists.

Directions: From Fort Atkinson, take Highway 26 south to Old State Trunk Highway 26. Follow Old STH 26 to Koshkonong Mounds Road. Turn right and follow this road to Indian Mounds Trail Park on the left side of the road, past Vinne Ha Ha Road.

Facilities: Hiking.

Johnson Creek Park (Rock River Park)

Also known as Rock River Park, this four-acre park on the Rock River is a popular fishing and boat-launching spot.

Directions: From Jefferson, take Highway 26 north to Johnson Creek. In Johnson Creek, take County B one mile west of Johnson Creek.

Facilities: Picnic tables, outhouses, boat landing.

Joy Park

Located on the shores of Spence Lake, picnickers come to one-acre Joy Park to enjoy its scenic setting.

Directions: From the junction of I-94 and County F just north of Concord, take County F north to the park.

Facilities: Picnic tables.

Kanow Park

Fishing the Rock River is the most popular activity at this 45-acre park just east of Ixonia. A large open area offers room for outdoor play.

Directions: From Watertown, take Highway 16 east past Ixonia to Rock River Road. Turn north on Rock River Road and proceed ¼ mile to the park.

Facilities: Picnic tables, picnic shelter, outhouses, playground.

McCoy Park

This picnic spot offers grills, tables and shade.

Directions: In Fort Atkinson, take Highway 12 to the west side of town. The park is off Highway 12.

Facilities: Picnic tables, toilets.

Pohlman Park

Planted with 1,000 white pine and white spruce trees in 1984, 10-acre Pohlman Park now attracts bird watchers, nature students and picnickers. The park is adjacent to the Glacial Drumlin State Trail.

Directions: From Jefferson, take Highway 18 east to Helenville. Continue past Helenville one mile on 18 to Duck Creek Road. The park is at the northwest corner of the junction.

Facilities: Picnic tables, picnic shelter, outhouses, playground.

Rock Lake Park

Upper and Lower Rock Lake parks are the most heavily used of Jefferson County's parks. Facilities at Upper Rock Lake Park include a hiking trail and a picnic area with grills. The Lower Rock Lake Park offers a boat launch on Rock Lake, swimming area, picnic area with grills and a playground.

Directions: From Lake Mills, take County B west about 1½ miles. To reach Lower Rock Lake Park, turn on Park Lane Road. To reach Upper Rock Lake Park, turn on Rock Lake Road and proceed ¼ mile to the park.

Facilities: Picnic tables, picnic shelter, outhouses, swimming, playground, boat landing.

Rome Pond Park

This 12-acre park offers boat access to Rome Pond and a spot to picnic; grills are provided. An adjacent wildlife area often brings visitors here.

Directions: From Fort Atkinson, take Highway 106 east to County F. Turn north and continue to Rome. In Rome, follow F east and travel ½ mile to the park.

Facilities: Picnic tables, picnic shelter, outhouses, boat landing.

Welcome Travelers Park

Softball and baseball are the most popular activities at this eight-acre park just north of Whitewater. The picnic area has a shelter and grills.

Directions: From the city of Whitewater in the northwest corner of Walworth County, take Highway 59 north one mile to the junction with County D.

Facilities: Picnic tables, picnic shelter, baseball, playground.

JUNEAU COUNTY

Contact: Juneau County Parks and Forestry
250 Oak St.
Mauston, WI 53948
(608) 847-9389

Hundreds of county parks provide picnic areas that serve both travelers and local residents.

Bass Hollow Recreation Area

Located in the southern portion of the county, Bass Hollow Recreation Area offers five miles of scenic walking trails and a picnic area. At 280 acres, it's Juneau County's largest county park.

Directions: Take I-90 to the Mauston exit at Highway 82. Go west on Highway 82 to Union Street and turn left. Follow Union Street to Highway 12-16 and go left, then right at County K. Go south five miles on County K to the park.

Facilities: Picnic tables, picnic shelter, outhouses, hiking.

Castle Rock Park

Situated on Castle Rock Flowage, Wisconsin's fourth largest inland body of water at 16,000 acres, Juneau County Castle Rock Park offers 300 wooded campsites (half with electricity), showers and a handicapped-accessible bathhouse. Water enthusiasts will find plenty to do—swimming at the supervised beach, boating, canoeing, waterskiing and fishing are all popular warm-weather activities. The park also provides grills and concessions.

Directions: Take Highway 58 to County G. Go east on County G about four miles to the park.

Facilities: Picnic tables, picnic shelter, outhouses, toilets, tent sites, trailer sites, swimming, beach, dressing rooms, hiking, playground, boat landing.

Kennedy Park

Just north of New Lisbon, Kennedy Park is a quiet spot to set up camp on the Lemonweir River. The park has 15 unmarked, primitive campsites, picnic tables and grills, and provides access to the river for fishing, swimming, canoeing and boating. White pine trees offer shade, and group campsites are available.

Directions: From I-90, take the New Lisbon exit to Highway 80. Take Highway 80 south to Highway 12-16 and turn right. Follow Highway 12-16 to County M, turn right, and go about four miles to the park.

Facilities: Picnic tables, picnic shelter, outhouses, tent sites, trailer sites, swimming, hiking, playground.

Oak Ridge Park

Oak Ridge Park offers seven miles of trails through county forest land for walking, cross-country skiing and hunting.

Directions: From I-90, take the New Lisbon exit to Highway 80. Take Highway 80 south to Highway 12-16 and turn right. Follow Highway 12-16 to County M, turn right, and go about seven miles to the park.

Facilities: Picnic shelter, outhouses, hiking, cross-country skiing.

Wilderness Park

The blue waters of 23,000-acre Petenwell Flowage draw visitors to the park for summer swimming, boating, sailing, canoeing, waterskiing and fishing. Wilderness Park offers 140 campsites (some with electricity), grills, a playground and hiking trails. Group campsites are available. The park's location on county forest land gives it a rustic character.

Directions: Take Highway 58 to Necedah and go east at Highway 21. Go 1½ miles on Highway 21 to County G. Take County G to 9th Street.

Facilities: Picnic tables, picnic shelter, outhouses, tent sites, trailer sites, swimming, beach, hiking, playground, boat landing.

KENOSHA COUNTY

Contact: Kenosha County
Department of Public Works
Park Division
P.O. Box 549
19600 - 75th St.
Bristol, WI 53104
(414) 653-1869

Brighton Dale Park

Brighton Dale Park, located 14 miles west of Kenosha, features a 45-hole championship golf course. The park also offers a fishing pond, nature trails, baseball diamonds and wooded picnic areas. Winter recreation opportunities include cross-country skiing on three groomed trails, ice fishing, sledding and ice skating.

Directions: Take Highway 75 just north from the junction of Highway 142 and Highway 75.

Facilities: Picnic tables, toilets, hiking, nature trails, cross-country skiing, baseball, golf, playground.

Bristol Woods Park

Hiking trails—cross-country ski trails in the winter—wind through the woodlands of this quiet 198-acre park. Picnic facilities with grills are provided.

Directions: From I-94, take County C west to County MB. Turn south and continue to the park.

Facilities: Picnic tables, picnic shelter, toilets, hiking, nature trails, cross-country skiing, playground.

Fox River Park

The Fox River meanders along the eastern boundary of the park, providing opportunities to canoe, boat and fish. Within the park's 149 acres, visitors will find tennis courts, softball diamonds, open lawn space for games, and picnic areas with grills. Winter activities include cross-country skiing through wooded terrain and a bermed sled slide with nighttime lighting.

Directions: Take I-94 to to Highway 50 and go west. Turn south at County F and continue on this road until you reach its intersection with County W, where the park is located.

Facilities: Picnic tables, picnic shelter, toilets, hiking, nature trails, cross-country skiing, baseball, tennis, playground, boat landing.

Kemper Center

Located along the shore of Lake Michigan in Kenosha, Kemper Center is a recreational facility often used for lawn concerts, art exhibits and weddings. Within the facility's 11 wooded acres are picnic tables, tennis courts and a handicapped-accessible fishing pier.

Directions: Located in the city of Kenosha, just east on Highway 50 from the intersection of Highway 50 and Highway 32.

Facilities: Picnic tables, toilets, tennis, playground.

Old Settlers' Park

Though it's the smallest Kenosha County park, Old Settlers' Park is one of the most popular for summer swimming and shady picnics. The sand beach on Paddock Lake receives heavy use. The park also offers a softball diamond, concessions and a spot to fish.

> **Directions:** Take I-94 to Highway 50. Go west seven miles on Highway 50, where the park is located.
>
> **Facilities:** Picnic tables, picnic shelter, toilets, swimming, beach, dressing rooms, baseball, playground.

Petrifying Springs Park

This 360-acre park, the largest in the county, offers year-round recreation. During the warm season, visitors can golf the 18-hole course, picnic with large groups, play softball, explore the nature trails, and ride horseback on the bridle trails. The winter months bring out cross-country skiers, ice skaters and sledders, who find relief from the cold in the park's warming shelter.

> **Directions:** From I-94, go east on Highway 50 to Highway 31. Take Highway 31 north to its intersection with County A, where the park is located. On summer weekends, access is at the intersection of Highway 31 and County JR.
>
> **Facilities:** Picnic tables, picnic shelter, toilets, hiking, nature trails, cross-country skiing, baseball, volleyball, golf, playground.

Silver Lake Park

Silver Lake Park's spacious sandy beach makes it a popular summer day getaway. The park also offers large picnic areas, concessions, softball and nature trails that take hikers past a scenic overview of Silver Lake. Both summer and winter anglers will appreciate Silver Lake for its walleye, northern pike, largemouth bass and pan fish. Other winter activities include a sledding hill and a four-kilometer cross-country ski trail.

> **Directions:** From I-94, go west on Highway 50. Turn south at County F and go one mile.
>
> **Facilities:** Picnic tables, picnic shelters, toilets, swimming, beach, dressing rooms, hiking, nature trails, cross-country skiing, baseball, volleyball, playground.

KEWAUNEE COUNTY

Contact: Kewaunee County Courthouse
613 Dodge St.
Kewaunee, WI 54216
(414) 388-4410

Bruemmer Park and Zoo

Located on the Kewaunee River, Bruemmer County Park is the largest and most used of the county's parks. A small zoo houses bears and deer, among other animals. Also within the park's 76 acres are large picnic areas, hiking trails and playground equipment. The Kewaunee River contains populations of trout and salmon.

Directions: From Highway 42 in Kewaunee, take Highway 29 west to the water tower, where County C forks off. Turn northwest on County C and travel to County F. The park is at the intersection.

Facilities: Picnic tables, picnic shelters, toilets, hiking, playground.

Bruemmerville Park

Heavily wooded and somewhat isolated, this two-acre park gives anglers a good spot to fish on the dam of Silver Creek. Though the facilities are limited to a few picnic tables and grills, the scenery makes for a peaceful summer picnic. In the winter, snowmobilers will find access to the county's snowmobile trail system.

Directions: From Algoma, take Freemont Street west to Willow Road. Turn north to the park.

Facilities: Picnic tables, picnic shelter, outhouses, playground.

East Alaska Lake Park

Boat landing on Alaska Lake, where anglers catch pan fish year-round.

Directions: From Algoma, take Highway 54 west to County D. Turn south and travel about 3½ miles to 7th Road. Travel east to the landing.

Facilities: Outhouses, boat landing.

Heidmann's Lake (Bolt Lake) Park

This one-acre park provides boaters and anglers with access to Heidmann's Lake, a small inland lake. There are two picnic tables and grills.

Directions: From Kewaunee, take Highway 42 south to the southern county line. Turn west on County BB. Continue eight miles to County Q. Turn north and travel one mile to Bolt Road. Then turn west and go ½ mile to the park.

Facilities: Picnic tables, outhouses, boat landing.

Highway 57 Wayside Park

Located on a primary route to Door County, Highway 57 Wayside Park offers travelers a spot to rest and picnic. Facilities include one picnic table and a grill.

Directions: From Green Bay, take Highway 57 north.
Facilities: Picnic table.

Krohn's Lake Park

Fishing for pan fish and boating are the main activities at this four-acre park five miles southwest of Algoma, though Krohn's Lake is also used for summer swimming. The park provides one grill, but no tables.
    Directions: From Algoma, take Highway 42 south to County K. Turn west and travel two miles to County KK. Turn south and continue to the park.
    Facilities: Toilets, swimming, boat landing.

Red River Park

The park's location on Green Bay and the Red River primarily attracts boaters and anglers in search of the bay's perch. A small sand beach can be used for swimming, and picnic facilities include a shelter, tables and grills.
    Directions: From Green Bay, take Highway 57 north. Continue two miles past Dyckesville. The park will be on the left.
    Facilities: Picnic tables, picnic shelter, toilets, swimming, beach, baseball, playground, boat landing.

Shea's Lake Park

Fishing, ice fishing and boating are the primary activities at this two-acre park on Shea's Lake, a small inland lake in the southwest corner of Kewaunee County. Visitors who don't have their own boat can rent one from nearby facilities. Picnic facilities are limited to one table and grill.
    Directions: From Kewaunee, take Highway 42 south to the southern county line. Turn west on County BB. Continue eight miles to County Q. Turn north and travel two miles to County KB. Turn west and go ½ mile to the park.
    Facilities: Picnic table, outhouses, boat landing.

West Alaska Lake Park

Icefishing is popular at this park on Alaska Lake, where anglers will find mostly pan fish. Only electric motors are allowed on the lake. The park also has a swimming beach, two picnic tables and a grill.
    Directions: From Algoma, take Highway 54 west to County D. Go south on County D about 3½ miles.
    Facilities: Picnic tables, outhouses, swimming, beach, boat landing.

LA CROSSE COUNTY

Contact: La Crosse County Parks Department
Courthouse
400 N. 4th St.
La Crosse, WI 54601
(608) 785-9770

Goose Island Park

This wooded island in the Mississippi River offers a unique setting and a wide range of outdoor activities, including camping, fishing, nature trail hiking, swimming, canoeing, bird watching, waterfowl hunting or just watching the sun set behind the Minnesota Bluffs. The backwaters around the island abound with fish, waterfowl and aquatic life. Within the park's 710 acres are more than 400 campsites (with electricity); showers are available. Visitors can rent canoes and boats, lounge on the sand beach, play basketball or volleyball, choose from 200 acres of picnic area and, in the winter, cross-country ski the island's woodlands. Group campsites are available.

> **Directions:** Take Highway 14-61 to Highway 35. Go south on Highway 35 to County GI and follow it west into the park.
> **Facilities:** Picnic tables, picnic shelters, outhouses, toilets, tent sites, trailer sites, swimming, beach, hiking, nature trails, cross-country skiing, volleyball, playground, boat landing.

Lake Neshonoc South Park

Located on the south shore of Lake Neshonoc, this park provides boat access, picnic tables and hiking trails. It is under development.

> **Directions:** From West Salem, take Tilson Street ¾ mile east.
> **Facilities:** Picnic tables, hiking, boat landing.

Mindoro Park

Originally a 120-acre hilly, wooded farm, Mindoro Park is being transformed into a wildlife habitat and nature study retreat. Forty thousand pine and walnut trees have been planted and an extensive system of nature trails winds through the park.

> **Directions:** From La Crosse, take Highway 53 north to County D. Follow County D to the park, just west of Mindoro.
> **Facilities:** Picnic tables, outhouses, hiking, nature trails, baseball, playground.

Nelson Park

Located on the tip of French Island, Nelson Park is the most popular boating and fishing access to Lake Onalaska, often used for sailing. The shaded park provides a good spot for picnicking and playing softball.

Directions: Take Highway 53-35 south through La Crosse to Clinton Street and go right. Follow Clinton Street to Bainbridge Street and go right again. Take a left on Goodard Street, which turns into Lakeshore Drive and leads directly into the park.

Facilities: Picnic tables, picnic shelter, outhouses, baseball, playground, boat landing.

Swarthout Park

Neshonoc Swarthout Park is situated on a high bank overlooking Lake Neshonoc. The park provides a spot to picnic and watch the waterskiers. Boats can be launched below at a boat landing.

Directions: From La Crosse, take Highway 16 east to the park, ½ mile east of West Salem on the highway.

Facilities: Picnic tables, picnic shelter, outhouses, swimming, volleyball, playground, boat landing.

Swarthout Brice Prairie Park

This neighborhood park offers large group picnic areas and opportunities to play tennis and volleyball. A boat launch on Lake Onalaska is across the street.

Directions: From La Crosse, take Highway 35-53 north to County Z. Go west on County Z to County ZB, where the park is located.

Facilities: Picnic tables, picnic shelter, outhouses, volleyball, tennis, playground, boat landing.

Veteran's Memorial Park

Bordered on one side by the La Crosse River and on the other by the Sparta-La Crosse bicycle trail, Veteran's Memorial Park has 100 campsites with electricity and free firewood, and a wide range of outdoor activity. Visitors can canoe and fish the river, bike and hike the trails, and play beach volleyball and shuffleboard. Picnickers have access to shelters and grills.

Directions: From La Crosse, take Highway 16 east about nine miles to the park.

Facilities: Picnic tables, picnic shelters, outhouses, toilets, tent sites, trailer sites, hiking, baseball, volleyball, playground, canoe landing.

LAFAYETTE COUNTY

Contact: Blackhawk Memorial Park
2995 County Y
Woodford, WI 53599
(608) 465-3390

Blackhawk Memorial Park

Dedicated to Chief Blackhawk and the Sac Indians and pioneer settlers who fought to protect their way of life here in the early 1800s, Blackhawk Memorial Park is now the site of the annual Bloody Lake Rendezvous. Primitive campsites sit either on the shores of the Pecatonica River or near its backwaters. The park offers a quiet place to fish and canoe.

> **Directions:** Take Highway 81 in Green County to County Y. Go west on County Y to the park in Woodford.

> **Facilities:** Picnic tables, outhouses, tent sites, trailer sites, baseball, playground, boat landing.

LANGLADE COUNTY

Contact: Langlade County Forestry Department
P.O. Box 460
Antigo, WI 54409
(715) 627-6300

Hunting River Wayside

This wayside provides walk-in access to the Hunting River, noted for its excellent supply of trout.

> **Directions:** From Antigo, go 15 miles north on Highway 45 to County T. Go east on County T five miles to the park.

> **Facilities:** Picnic tables, outhouses.

Langlade County Bow and Gun Range

South of Antigo, this park offers 25-, 50-, 100-, 200- and 300-yard small and large bore rifle and bow ranges.

> **Directions:** From Antigo, go south two miles on Highway 45 to Sunnyside Road. Go east one mile to the park.

> **Facilities:** Picnic tables, outhouses.

Moose Lake Boat Landing

Anglers will find brown trout and pan fish in this deep, cold lake. The park provides a boat landing, used primarily by motor boats, and picnic tables.

Directions: From Antigo, go south five miles on Highway 45 to Highway 47. Go east on Highway 47 six miles, north on County S two miles, and then left on Park Road.

Facilities: Picnic tables, outhouses, boat landing.

Otter Lake Wayside

This wayside provides a rest and picnic spot along Highway 45-47, and fishing and boat access to Otter Lake.

Directions: Go north from Elcho one mile on Highway 45-47.

Facilities: Picnic tables, outhouses, boat landing.

Post Lake Wayside

Post Lake, which hosts populations of muskellunge, walleye, small and largemouth bass and northern pike, has open fishing waters year-round. The wayside provides picnic tables and a boat launch.

Directions: Take Highway 45-47 to County K in Elcho. Go east on County K four miles to the park.

Facilities: Picnic tables, outhouses, boat landing.

Summit Lake Park

Summit Lake County Park has a roped-off swimming area, playground and picnic tables.

Directions: Take Highway 45-47 north from Antigo. The lake is on the west side of the highway in Summit Lake.

Facilities: Picnic tables, outhouses, swimming, dressing rooms, playground.

Veterans Memorial Park

A five-acre, 3,000-specimen arboretum is attached to the park's nature trail, which takes hikers across a bog and around several small lakes. Campers can choose from 41 sites, most with electricity. The park is located on Jack Lake, which provides opportunities to swim and launch nonmotorized boats.

Directions: Take Highway 45-47 north 12 miles from Antigo to County J. Follow County J east three miles to the park.

Facilities: Picnic tables, picnic shelter, outhouses, toilets, tent sites, trailer sites, swimming, beach, hiking, nature trails, volleyball, boat landing.

LINCOLN COUNTY

Contact: Lincoln County Forestry, Land
and Parks Department
1106 E. 8th St.
Merrill, WI 54452
(715) 536-0327

Camp New Wood Recreation Area

The Wisconsin River and four miles of the Ice Age Trail run through Camp New Wood Recreation Area. Eight campsites are available and picnic areas are equipped with grills. Bicyclists will want to explore the hilly scenery along Highway 107, which borders the park.

Directions: Take Highway 107 north from Merrill about eight miles to the park.

Facilities: Picnic tables, picnic shelter, outhouses, tent sites, trailer sites, hiking, playground, boat landing.

Hay Meadow Wayside

This wayside is used by area residents for picnicking and by weary travelers for resting.

Directions: Take Highway 17 north from Merrill 10 miles. Turn left on Old 17.

Facilities: Picnic tables, outhouses.

Otter Lake Recreation Area

A series of old logging roads now used for hiking winds through this hilly, isolated park on Otter Lake. The quiet park has 25 campsites, grills, cross-country ski trails, a swimming beach and a boat landing.

Directions: Take Highway 51 north from Merrill to County S and go east. Follow County S to Town Hall Road and continue east to Grundy Road. Go north on Grundy Road to Bear Trail Road, and east on Bear Trail Road to Otter Lake Road.

Facilities: Picnic tables, outhouses, tent sites, trailer sites, swimming, beach, dressing rooms, hiking, nature trails, cross-country skiing, boat landing.

Tug Lake Recreation Area

Tug Lake has a sand swimming beach, picnic area with a shelter and grills, and a playground.

Directions: From Merrill, take County K north 7½ miles to Tug Lake Road.
Facilities: Picnic tables, picnic shelter, outhouses, swimming, beach, dressing rooms, playground.

MANITOWOC COUNTY

Contact: Manitowoc County Planning
and Park Commission
1701 Michigan Ave.
Manitowoc, WI 54220
(414) 683-4185

Bullhead Lake Public Access

Boat landing and fishing pier on Bullhead Lake, noted for sizable populations of walleye, perch, crappie and bluegill.
  Directions: From Manitowoc, take County JJ west to the west county line. When County JJ turns north, continue for ½ mile to Bullhead Lane, which leads directly to the lake.
  Facilities: Outhouses, boat landing.

Carstens Lake Public Access

Boat landing and fishing pier on 20-acre Carstens Lake. The lake has been stocked with northern pike and bass.
  Directions: From Manitowoc, take Highway 42 south three miles to Carstens Lake Road. Turn east and continue ½ mile.
  Facilities: Outhouses, boat landing.

Cedar Lake Public Access

Boat landing and fishing pier on 139-acre Cedar Lake, the largest inland lake in Manitowoc County. It hosts populations of northern pike, bass, perch, crappie and bluegills. This site also has a picnic area.
  Directions: From Manitowoc, take Highway 42 south 10 miles to County XX. Turn west and go five miles to Cedar Lake Road. Turn south and go ¼ mile.
  Facilities: Picnic tables, boat landing.

Cherney Maribel Caves Park

A rugged limestone cliffline separates the wooded upland area from the lowland area next to the West Twin River. Visitors can poke their heads into the small caves (15-20 feet) and openings in the rock layers. The upland section of this 75-acre park provides opportunities to picnic and hike. Trout can be fished from the river.

Directions: From the I-43 exit at Maribel, go east on County Z ¼ mile to County R. Turn north and go ½ mile.

Facilities: Picnic tables, picnic shelter, outhouses, hiking, playground.

English Lake Public Access

Though used primarily for fishing and boating access to 51-acre English Lake, the site also contains a picnic area with grills. Anglers will appreciate the 70-foot T-shaped pier, where they can cast their lines for walleye, largemouth bass and pan fish.

Directions: From Manitowoc, take Highway 42 south 2½ miles to English Lake Road. Turn west and go two miles to Brunner Road. Travel ½ mile to the entrance road to English Lake.

Facilities: Picnic tables, outhouses, boat landing.

Gass Lake Public Access

Boat landing and fishing pier on 6½-acre Gass Lake, best known for largemouth bass.

Directions: From Manitowoc, take Highway 42 south 1½ miles to Gass Lake Road. Turn east and go one mile.

Facilities: Boat landing only.

Harpt Lake Public Access

Boat landing and fishing pier on 20-acre Harpt Lake, noted for its populations of walleye, largemouth bass and black crappie. Northern pike, perch, bluegill and rock bass are also found here.

Directions: From the I-43 exit at Maribel, go east 2½ miles on Highway 147 to Harpt Lake Road. Turn north and proceed two miles to North Lake Road. Turn west and continue ⅛ mile.

Facilities: Boat landing only.

Hartlaub Lake Public Access

Boat landing and fishing pier on 38-acre Hartlaub Lake, known for its populations of northern pike, bass, walleye and pan fish.

Directions: From Manitowoc, take Highway 42 south two miles to Hartlaub Lake Road. Turn east and go one mile to the lake.

Facilities: Boat landing only.

Horseshoe Lake Park

Predominantly used for fishing, the 19-acre horseshoe-shaped lake hosts populations of rainbow trout, largemouth bass, crappie, bluegill, northern pike and perch. Only nonmotorized boats are allowed on the lake. Horseshoe Lake Park also contains several picnic areas with grills and a playground. Visitors should keep their eyes open for some of the more hidden, beautiful spots in the park.

Directions: From Manitowoc, take Highway 42 south 10 miles to County XX. Turn west and go three miles.

Facilities: Picnic tables, outhouses, playground, boat landing.

Long Lake Park

Anglers can fish 117-acre Long Lake from a boat, from the handicapped-accessible fishing pier or from shore, where weeping willows lean into the water. The lake's populations of northern pike, largemouth bass, walleye, perch, white bass, bullhead, crappie, bluegill and pumpkinseed make it a popular spot year-round. The park also offers a picnic area with grills and a playground.

Directions: From Reedsville, take Highway 10 west to the county line. Turn south on Long Lake Road. Go 2½ miles to West Lake Road. Turn east and travel ¼ mile to the park.

Facilities: Picnic tables, outhouses, playground, boat landing.

Lower Cato Falls Park

Hikers will appreciate the scenery along the nature trails in this 84-acre park, where the Manitowoc River flows through a narrow gorge and into a small falls. While the lower level area remains in its natural state, the upland portion of the park, accessible by stairs, provides picnic tables, grills and playground equipment. Anglers will find rainbow trout in the Manitowoc River.

Directions: From Manitowoc, travel six miles west on County JJ.

Facilities: Picnic tables, outhouses, hiking, nature trails, playground.

Pigeon Lake Public Access

Boat landing and fishing pier on 77-acre Pigeon Lake, best known for walleye and northern pike. Waterskiing and boating are popular activities here.

Directions: From Manitowoc, take Highway 42 south seven miles to County F. Turn west and travel 2½ miles to Pigeon Lake Road. Turn north and go ¾ mile to the access.

Facilities: Boat landing only.

Shoe Lake Public Access

Boat landing for nonmotorized boats on nine-acre Shoe Lake. Anglers will find bluegill, largemouth bass, green sunfish, pumpkinseed, black crappie, suckers, bullhead and an occasional northern pike.

Directions: From Manitowoc, take Highway 42 nine miles south to County X. Turn west and proceed seven miles to Lax Chapel Road. Turn south and go ¼ mile to Shoe Lake Road. Turn west and continue to the access.

Facilities: Boat landing only.

Silver Lake Park

This 12-acre wayside park contains a picnic area with a shelter, tables and grills, and a boat launch for nonmotorized boats. Silver Lake spans 55 acres and hosts primarily rough fish, though lucky anglers may find largemouth bass, northern pike, perch or pan fish.

Directions: From Manitowoc, take Highway 151 west one mile.

Facilities: Picnic tables, picnic shelter, outhouses, boat landing.

Spring Lake Public Access

Boat landing for nonmotorized boats on eight-acre Spring Lake, where anglers will find northern pike, largemouth bass and bluegill.

Directions: From Manitowoc, take Highway 42 south seven miles to County F. Turn west and go three miles to Spring Lake Road. Turn south and go ½ mile to East Spring Lake Road. Turn west and continue to the landing.

Facilities: Boat landing only.

Tuma Lake Public Access

Boat landing on 15-acre Tuma Lake. The lake provides good fishing for walleye as well as bass, bluegill, perch, black crappie and northern pike.

Directions: From the I-43 exit at Maribel, turn east on Highway 147. Go 2½ miles to Harpt Lake Road. Turn north and go one mile to West Tuma Lake Road. Turn west and travel ¼ mile to Lake Road. Then turn south and continue for ⅛ mile.

Facilities: Boat landing only.

Walla Hi Park

Several hiking trails meander through this park's kettle moraine landscape, through woodlands and open expanses, and past small springs and streams. The same trails can be used for cross-country skiing during the winter months. Snowmobile trails are also available. Walla Hi County Park's 160 acres include picnic areas with grills, a playground, an abandoned fish hatchery and a spring-fed pond where anglers can try their luck.

Directions: From Kiel, travel east on Rockville Road two miles to South Cedar Lake Road. Turn south and go one mile to Mueller Road. Turn west and go ¼ mile to the park.

Facilities: Picnic tables, outhouses, hiking, nature trails, cross-country skiing, playground.

West Twin River Public Access

Located on a wide bend in the West Twin River near Shoto, this site is used primarily for boat and fishing access. Anglers can fish from boat or pier for trout, salmon, northern pike, catfish and bass. Picnic tables are also provided.

Directions: From Two Rivers, take County VV west two miles to the park.

Facilities: Picnic tables, boat landing.

Wilke Lake Public Access

A boat landing on 97-acre Wilke Lake, this site also contains a picnic area with grills. The lake is most noted for its largemouth bass, northern pike and walleye.

Directions: From Manitowoc, take Highway 42 south eight miles to Point Creek Road. Turn west and go five miles to Wilke Lake Road. Turn north and travel ⅛ mile to the water's edge.

Facilities: Picnic tables, outhouses, boat landing.

MARATHON COUNTY

Contact: Wausau/Marathon County
Park Department
County Courthouse
500 Forest St.
Wausau, WI 54403
(715) 847-5235

Amco Park

This natural area on the Big Rib River is a nice spot to picnic or fish.

Directions: From Wausau, take Highway 29 west nine miles to Highway 107. Turn north and go 10 miles to Highway F. Turn west and travel seven miles to the park.

Facilities: Picnic tables, outhouses, playground.

Ashley Park

One hundred sixty acres of undeveloped land.

Directions: From Wausau, take Highway 51 south 16 miles to Highway 34. Turn west and go ¼ mile to Highway DB. Turn south and travel one mile to Highway C. Turn east and go 1½ miles to Rozak Road. Turn right on Rozak Road and continue two miles to the park.

Facilities: None.

Big Eau Pleine Park

The largest park in the Marathon County Park System, Big Eau Pleine Park contains more than 2,000 acres of woodland peninsula on the north shore of Big Eau Pleine Reservoir. Most of the land is undeveloped, supporting white-tail deer, black bear, raccoon and partridge. Two campgrounds offer a total of 106 campsites. Other facilities include three boat landings, a swimming beach, nine miles of hiking and biking trails, and summer-use bridle trails.

Directions: From Wausau, take Highway 51 south 12 miles to Highway 153. Turn west and travel eight miles to Eau Pleine Park Road. Turn south and go 3½ miles to the park entrance.

Facilities: Picnic tables, picnic shelters, outhouses, tent sites, trailer sites, swimming, beach, dressing rooms, hiking, nature trails, cross-country skiing, playground, boat landing.

Big Rapids Park

Big Rapids Park provides a spot to swim, fish and picnic on the Big Eau Pleine River. Wildflowers flourish along the banks of the river.

Directions: From Wausau, take Highway 51 south three miles to Highway N. Turn west on N and travel 23 miles to Highway 97. Turn south and go four miles to Big Rapids Road. Turn west and continue one mile to the park.

Facilities: Picnic tables, picnic shelter, outhouses, swimming, beach, dressing rooms, playground.

Bluegill Bay Park

This 96-acre park on Lake Wausau draws anglers, boaters and outdoors enthusiasts. In addition to hiking trails, Bluegill Bay has volleyball courts, horseshoe pits and picnic facilities.

Directions: From Wausau, take Highway 51 south two miles to Highway NN. Turn east and go ¼ mile to Highway N (Rib Mountain Drive). Turn south and go ½ mile to Oriole Lane, then travel east ½ mile on Oriole to the park. Or go south on Rib Mountain Drive one mile to Cloverland Lane, traveling east ½ mile on Cloverland to the park.

Facilities: Picnic tables, picnic shelter, outhouses, hiking, volleyball, boat landing.

Cherokee Park

Just upstream from Big Rapids Park, 69-acre Cherokee Park provides opportunities to fish, hike and picnic under a reservable 1930s shelter.

Directions: From Wausau, take Highway 51 south three miles to County N, then travel west on County N 30 miles to the park. Or from Wausau, take Highway 29 west 28 miles to County F, and travel south three miles on County F to the park.

Facilities: Picnic tables, picnic shelter, outhouses, hiking, playground.

Wazee Lake in Jackson County is Wisconsin's deepest lake and a popular spot for scuba diving.

D.C. Everest Park

Visitors who show up on Wednesdays or Sundays during the summer might catch one of the local water-ski shows at this five-acre park on Lake Wausau. When the waters are open, D.C. Everest Park offers a boat launch and opportunities to fish. Other facilities include a picnic area and hiking trails.

Directions: In Wausau, take 3rd Avenue south of Thomas Street ½ mile to the park.

Facilities: Picnic tables, picnic shelter, outhouses, hiking, boat landing.

Dells of the Eau Claire Park

The rock gorge carved by the continuous rush of the Eau Claire River rapids creates a wild and scenic backdrop for camping, hiking and picnicking. The campground has 26 sites, some with electricity, and separate group sites. A quieter stretch of river away from the rapids and falls is used as a swimming area.

Directions: From Wausau, take County Z east 14 miles to County Y. Go north on County Y 1½ miles.

Facilities: Picnic tables, picnic shelter, outhouses, tent sites, trailer sites, swimming, beach, dressing rooms, hiking, playground.

Duane L. Corbin Shooting Range

This 101-acre park contains 25-, 50-, 100- and 200-yard pit-targeted ranges, covered shooting points, hand-trap and archery ranges.

Directions: From Wausau, take Highway 51 south three miles to County N. Turn west and travel two miles to County KK. Turn south and continue six miles to the park.

Facilities: None.

Marathon Park

A forest of white pine shelters the hiking trails and 35-unit campground at this 78-acre urban park. Marathon Park is quite diverse, offering a wading pool, curling rink, jogging track, miniature train and, in the winter, a sledding hill and indoor ice for hockey and figure skating. Other facilities include tennis courts, three baseball diamonds, volleyball courts and picnic grills.

Directions: In Wausau, take Highway 52 north to Exit Highway 52 east. Travel east on Highway 52 (Stewart Avenue) ¼ mile to the park, located at the junction with 17th Avenue.

Facilities: Picnic tables, picnic shelter, toilets, tent sites, trailer sites, hiking, baseball, volleyball, tennis, playground.

Mission Lake Park

One of the few natural lakes in Marathon County, Mission Lake draws the angler with its unpolluted waters and populations of pan fish, bass, northern pike and muskellunge. The park has a sand beach for swimming and sunning, and a picnic area overlooking the lake.

Directions: From Wausau, take Highway 51 south 12 miles to Highway 153. Turn east and travel 15 miles to County Y. Turn north and go one mile to Crooked Lake Road. Turn east and travel 1½ miles to the park.

Facilities: Picnic tables, picnic shelter, outhouses, swimming, beach, dressing rooms, hiking, nature trails, volleyball, playground, boat landing.

Rib Falls Park

Picnickers, hikers and anglers will enjoy the small, scenic falls at this 315-acre park on the Big Rib River.

Directions: From Wausau, take Highway 29 west 13 miles to County S. Go north on County S two miles to its intersection with County U.

Facilities: Picnic tables, picnic shelter, outhouses, hiking, playground.

Sunny Vale Park

Sunny Vale Park's 284 acres, located on Sunny Vale Lake just west of Wausau, include a swimming beach, picnic facilities and volleyball courts. Visitors also have opportunities to hike and fish the lake.

Directions: In Wausau, take Stewart Avenue (Highway 29) west three miles to 72nd Avenue. Travel south ½ mile on 72nd Avenue to the park.

Facilities: Picnic tables, picnic shelter, outhouses, swimming, beach, dressing rooms, hiking, volleyball.

MARINETTE COUNTY

Contact: Marinette County Forestry and
Outdoor Recreation Office
Courthouse
1926 Hall Ave.
P.O. Box 320
Marinette, WI 54143
(715) 732-7530

Bear Point Boat Landing

Boat landing on the Menominee River.

Directions: Take Highway 141 to Highway 180 near Wausaukee and turn east. Follow Highway 180 six miles to the boat landing.

Facilities: Outhouses, boat landing.

Cox Boat Landing

Boat landing on the Menominee River.

Directions: From Marinette, take Highway 180 northwest. The landing is ½ mile northwest of the junction with County T.

Facilities: Boat landing only.

Crystal Springs Wayside Park

Stop to enjoy the scenery and an afternoon picnic at this five-acre wayside park on the Menominee River along Highway 180.

Directions: From Marinette, take Highway 180 northwest four miles to the park.

Facilities: Picnic tables.

Dave's Falls Park

Named after a log driver who died in a log jam on the wild Pike River, Dave's Falls Park offers a scenic view of the falls as they pound through little canyons and rock outcroppings. The best time to see the falls is morning, when the sun shines directly into the falls from the east. A picnic area and playground are provided.

Directions: From Wausaukee, travel north on Highway 141. The park is ½ mile south of Amberg off 141.

Facilities: Picnic tables, outhouses, hiking, playground.

Dolan Lake Park

Boat landing on Dolan Lake in the town of Athelstane.

Directions: From Wausaukee, travel north on Highway 141 to Amberg. In Amberg, turn west on Down Dam Road. Continue seven miles to Dolan Lake Road. Turn north and continue to the park.

Facilities: Outhouses, boat landing.

Goodman Park

This scenic spot on the Peshtigo River features 100-foot-high red pine trees, a bridge over Strong Falls and two day-use lodges built by the Civilian Conservation Corps. Goodman Park's 240 acres encompass 15 campsites, picnic areas, and hiking and cross-country ski trails. Anglers can also fish for trout on the Peshtigo.

Directions: From Wausaukee, travel west on County C for 20 miles to Parkway Road. Turn south and go nine miles to Goodman Park Road. Turn northwest and travel two miles to the park.

Facilities: Picnic tables, picnic shelters, outhouses, tent sites, trailer sites, hiking, cross-country skiing, playground.

Lake Noquebay Park

Children can swim safely on the south shore of Lake Noquebay, where the water is shallow and a bathhouse is located close to the beach. Visitors to the park's historic Works Progress Administration lodge will appreciate the view of the lake through a corridor of trees. Picnic facilities and a boat landing are provided.

Directions: From the intersection of Highway 141 and County W in Crivitz, take County W east two miles to County GG. Follow County GG four miles northeast.

Facilities: Picnic tables, picnic shelter, outhouses, toilets, swimming, beach, dressing rooms, baseball, volleyball, playground, boat landing.

Left Foot Lake Park

Located three miles south of Crivitz, this park offers a swimming beach on 39-acre Left Foot Lake.

Directions: From Highway 141 in Crivitz, go west ¼ mile on County W to Left Foot Lake Road. Go south 2½ miles on this road to the park.

Facilities: Swimming, beach.

Little River Boat Landing

Boat landing on Green Bay.

Directions: From Highway 141 in Marinette, take County T to County B. Take County B south two miles from Marinette to the park.

Facilities: Outhouses, boat landing.

Long Slide Falls Wayside Park

At this park, take a scenic hike and view the beautiful 50-foot Long Slide Falls of the Pemebonwon River.

Directions: From Pembine, go north on Highway 141 four miles to Morgan Park Road. Turn east and travel two miles to the park.

Facilities: Hiking.

McClintock Park

McClintock Park's four wooden bridges cross the rapids of the upper Peshtigo River, offering a good backdrop for taking pictures and picnicking. The 320-acre park also has 10 campsites.

Directions: From Wausaukee, travel west on County C for 20 miles to Parkway Road. Turn south and go 13 miles to the park.

Facilities: Picnic tables, picnic shelter, outhouses, tent sites, trailer sites.

Menominee River Park

Because it gets little use, Menominee River Park and its waters have remained relatively pristine. Picnic here, enjoy the river view, or launch a boat.

Directions: Take Highway 180 north 13 miles from Marinette to its intersection with County X.

Facilities: Picnic tables, picnic shelter, outhouses, hiking, playground, boat landing.

Michaelis Park

Two-acre Michaelis Park offers swimming in Green Bay and a spot to picnic.

Directions: From Highway 141 in Marinette, take County T to County B. Take County B south two miles from Marinette to the park.

Facilities: Picnic tables, outhouses, swimming, beach, playground.

Morgan Park

The 125-foot bluffs at one end of Morgan Park offer visitors a scenic overlook of Timms Lake, located six miles east of Pembine. The 160-acre park has 36 campsites with electricity, a lodge, opportunities to fish and swim, and a boat landing.

Directions: From the junction of Highway 8 and Highway 141, take Highway 141 north past Pembine to Kremlin Road. Turn east and travel six miles to Timm's Lake Road. Turn north and go one mile.

Facilities: Picnic tables, picnic shelter, outhouses, tent sites, swimming, dressing rooms, hiking, playground, boat landing.

Newton Lake Park

This tiny park offers swimming on Newton Lake, 12 miles northwest of Crivitz.

Directions: From Crivitz, travel west on County A through its curve to the north. Continue for a total of 15 miles on County A to Orlando Road. Turn west and go one mile to Newton Lake Road. Turn north and go ¾ mile to the park.

Facilities: Outhouses, swimming, beach.

Old Veteran's Lake Campground

Oak trees, sand beaches and a peaceful lake characterize this 80-acre park in the town of Stephenson. Sixteen campsites are available, and a hiking trail circles the lake. Motors are not allowed on Veteran's Lake.

Directions: From Wausaukee, take Highway 141 south to Middle Inlet. Turn west on County X and travel 16 miles to Parkway Road. Turn north and travel 3¼ miles to the park.

Facilities: Picnic tables, outhouses, tent sites, trailer sites, swimming, beach, hiking, playground.

Salor Boat Landing

Boat landing on the Menominee River in the town of Niagara.

Directions: From Pembine, travel north on Highway 141 to Kremlin Road. Turn east and go 10 miles to Rattie Road. Turn east and go six miles to the landing.

Facilities: Boat landing only.

Thunder Mountain Park

Thunder Mountain Park is an undeveloped 160-acre area in the town of Stephenson. According to legend, the Indians believed the mountain was magical. Some say the mountain allows footsteps at the top of the hill to be heard near the bottom. The park provides scenic views, peace and quiet.

Directions: From Crivitz, take County W west 14½ miles to Cauldron Falls Road. Turn north and go three miles to Thunder Mountain Road. Turn west and go one mile to the mountain.

Facilities: None.

Twelve Foot Falls Park

Peaceful and out of the way, Twelve Foot Falls Park is nestled in the county's largest forest just south of Dunbar. The falls is one of a string of falls on the Pike River. Campers can choose from 12 rugged campsites near the reflecting pool of the falls. Anglers can fish the Pike River.

Directions: From the junction of Highway 141 and Highway 8, take Highway 8 west six miles to Lily Lake Road. Turn south and go two miles to Twin Lake Road. Turn west and go ½ mile to Twelve Foot Falls Road. Turn south and go ½ mile to the park.

Facilities: Picnic tables, outhouses, tent sites, hiking.

Twin Bridges Park

Twin Bridges Park is the place to be for the Marinette County social camping scene. This park, less rustic than the others, receives heavy use for water-skiing and powerboating on the Peshtigo River's High Falls Flowage. Campers can choose from 62 sites with electricity and swim, lounge on the beach and picnic.

Directions: From Wausaukee, take Highway 141 south to Middle Inlet. Turn west on County X and travel 16 miles to Parkway Road. Turn north and travel ¼ mile to the park.

Facilities: Picnic tables, outhouses, tent sites, trailer sites, swimming, beach, dressing rooms, playground.

Twin Creeks Boat Landing

Boat landing on the Menominee River.

Directions: From Marinette, take Highway 180 northeast six miles to the landing.

Facilities: Boat landing only.

Twin Islands Wayside Park

Travelers on Highway 180 can stop to rest or picnic at this wayside park on the Menominee River.

Directions: From Marinette, take Highway 180 northeast 14 miles.
Facilities: Picnic tables.

Veteran's Memorial Park

The bridge over the Thunder River falls is the main attraction of this 320-acre park, where visitors will find 15 wooded campsites, picnic facilities and opportunities to hike. Area anglers often fish the reflecting pool at the bottom of the falls for trout.

> **Directions:** From Crivitz, take County W west 12 miles to Parkway Road. Turn north and travel three miles to the park.
> **Facilities:** Picnic tables, outhouses, tent sites, trailer sites, hiking.

MARQUETTE COUNTY

Contact: Marquette County Clerk's Office
P.O. Box 186
Montello, WI 53949
(608) 297-9114

John Muir Memorial Park

John Muir Memorial Park is tucked away in the country on 80 acres of the boyhood home of environmental pioneer John Muir. The park offers a partly graveled nature trail, picnic tables and a baseball diamond. The trail encircles 25-acre Ennis Lake and crosses three bridges. Fishing and canoeing are popular activities on this lake.

> **Directions:** From the southern county line, take Highway 51 to County O. Go east on County O to County F and go north to the park.
> **Facilities:** Picnic tables, outhouses, hiking, nature trails, baseball.

MENOMINEE COUNTY

There are no county parks in Menominee County.

MILWAUKEE COUNTY

Contact: Milwaukee County Department
of Parks, Recreation and Culture
9480 Watertown Plank Road
Wauwatosa, WI 53226
(414) 257-6100

Note: Milwaukee County has 131 parks, some of which are quite small. The following list describes only the major parks, beaches and natural areas. For more information or a complete listing, contact Milwaukee County Department of Parks, Recreation and Culture.

Bradford Beach

Featuring 19 miles of sand beach, this park on the shore of Lake Michigan offers concessions, in-line skating, sand volleyball and a 10-kilometer jogging trail, which loops through the park and continues along the lakeshore.

Directions: In Milwaukee, take I-794 east to Lincoln Memorial Drive. Turn north and travel along the lake to the entrance.

Facilities: Picnic tables, toilets, swimming, beach, volleyball, playground.

Brown Deer Park

This 367-acre site features the premium golf course of Milwaukee's county park system. One of the top 10 public courses in the country, the 18-hole, 6,425-yard, par 71 course is also the home of the Greater Milwaukee Open. It provides a driving range, golf lessons and a restaurant. Other recreational activities in Brown Deer Park include fishing, baseball, sand volleyball, tennis, soccer, cross-country skiing and ice skating on the lagoon. For relaxation, visitors can enjoy a picnic in one of the eight designated picnic areas or enjoy a free movie in the park during the summer months. The Brown Deer Park Clubhouse, a boathouse with fireplace, is available for rent.

Directions: In Milwaukee, exit I-43 at Good Hope Road. Turn west on Good Hope Road and travel 1½ miles.

Facilities: Picnic tables, shelter, toilets, cross-country skiing, baseball, volleyball, tennis, golf, playground.

Cudahy Nature Preserve

Visitors to this 42-acre nature preserve can enjoy a stroll along several nature and hiking trails. Dogs are allowed and toilets are available by prior request.

Directions: Exit I-43 at the airport exit and continue to Howell Avenue. Travel south on Howell Avenue to E. College Avenue. Turn east and continue to the preserve.

Facilities: Toilets, hiking, nature trails.

Doctors Park

One of Milwaukee's county parks that allows dogs, this site offers 49 acres of parkway on Lake Michigan. A path leads to the beach on the northeastern end of Milwaukee County.

Directions: In Milwaukee, take I-794 east to Lincoln Memorial Drive. Travel north on Lincoln Memorial Drive, which turns into Lake Drive.

Facilities: Picnic tables, toilets, swimming, beach, playground.

Dretzka Park

This 326-acre park offers two designated picnic areas, a rugby field, cross-country skiing and sand volleyball. It also provides an 18-hole golf course with championship layout, a driving range, golf lessons and a restaurant. For special occasions, visitors can rent Dretzka Park Chalet, with a fireplace and an alpine atmosphere, or Dretzka Park Clubhouse, which has a view of the golf course.

Directions: In Milwaukee, take Highway 45 north to the interchange with Highway 145. Travel north on Highway 145.

Facilities: Picnic tables, picnic shelter, cross-country skiing, golf, playground.

Grant Park

The Lake Michigan shoreline at this park provides one of the best beaches in the county. Offering 381 acres of parkway, the site also features two boat launches, fishing on the lake and Friday-night fish fries at the park. Nine designated picnic areas, six tennis courts, baseball, sand volleyball, a bike trail and a recreation program are provided. Golfers can enjoy a high-quality 18-hole golf course that offers night golf and a restaurant. The Grant Park Clubhouse, a two-story historic farm house overlooking Lake Michigan and the golf course, is available for rent, along with an overnight lodge that sleeps 21 people and has a fireplace and kitchen.

Directions: In Milwaukee, take Highway 45 south from I-94. Follow Highway 45 to Layton Avenue. Turn east and travel to Lake Drive. Take Lake Drive south to the park.

Facilities: Picnic tables, toilets, swimming, beach, baseball, tennis, golf, playground, boat landings.

Greenfield Park

In this park, a lagoon and its three islands provide a scenic site for ice skating in the winter. A pavilion, which can be rented, has a scenic view. The 295-acre park provides a family water recreation area, swimming pools, slides, water sports and fishing on the lagoon. Visitors can enjoy a fish fry on Friday nights. There are also eight designated picnic areas, fitness trails, a bike trail, running track, baseball and sand volleyball, along with a high-quality 18-hole golf course with a restaurant.

Directions: In Milwaukee, take Highway 45 (894) south to Greenfield Avenue. Turn west and go ¼ mile.

Facilities: Picnic tables, toilets, swimming, hiking, baseball, golf, playground.

Lake Park

The northern end of a string of shoreline parks in downtown Milwaukee, 140.3-acre Lake Park is also the northern end of a 10-kilometer jogging trail that begins near War Memorial Art Center. One of the county parks that allows dogs, the park also offers six designated picnic areas, 4.6 miles of bike trail, an exercise trail, a running track, five tennis courts, a soccer field, a rugby field and a lawn bowling green. For beginning golfers, the park contains a pitch-and-putt, par 3, 18-hole golf course with night golf. The park also features Lake Park Bistro, an excellent restaurant on a bluff overlooking Lake Michigan with a French-themed continental menu.

Directions: In Milwaukee, take I-94 (794) east to Lincoln Memorial Drive. Travel north along the lake to the entrance.

Facilities: Picnic tables, toilets, baseball, tennis, golf, playground.

Lincoln Park

Located on the Milwaukee River, this 312-acre park provides access to a bike trail that connects north and south Milwaukee. The site also has six designated picnic areas, a pool with a water slide, tennis courts and ice skating on the lagoon. Facilities are also provided for baseball, soccer, basketball and football. Visitors can rent a pavilion with a view of the Milwaukee River or enjoy a day on the high-quality 9-hole golf course, which includes a restaurant.

Directions: In Milwaukee, take I-43 north to Hampton Avenue. Turn west to the park.

Facilities: Picnic tables, toilets, swimming, baseball, tennis, golf, playground.

McKinley Beach

The shore of Lake Michigan offers a sand swimming beach, along with fishing opportunites, at this park. A fish-cleaning station is also provided. Visitors can play sand volleyball or tennis, or jog along a 10-kilometer trail that runs through the park and continues along the shoreline.

Directions: In Milwaukee, take I-94 (794) east to Lincoln Memorial Drive. Travel north to the beach.

Facilities: Picnic tables, toilets, swimming, beach, volleyball, playground.

McKinley Marina

This site is a boater's paradise, with a marina, 655 boat slip rentals, a boat launch and sailing lessons, plus occasional fishing charters. For the nonboater, the park provides a 2.6-mile trail and concessions at Roundhouse Deli, along with access to the 10-kilometer lakeshore jogging trail and the "76" Bike Trail.

Directions: Directly adjacent to McKinley Beach (see listing above).
Facilities: Boat landing only.

Mitchell Park

The major attraction at this park is the Mitchell Park Horticultural Conservatory, also known as The Domes. The three glass-walled domes consist of the Arid Dome, with a desert setting that features a collection of cacti; the Tropical Dome, which features a waterfall and 750 species of plants; and the Show Dome, which is known for its floral shows throughout the year. The domes can be rented, along with a pavilion in the park on the lagoon's northern shore. Visitors can ice skate on the lagoon in the winter. The 60-acre park also contains three designated picnic areas, four tennis courts, basketball courts, a football field, sand volleyball and free movies on Friday nights during the summer.

Directions: In Milwaukee, exit I-94 at 26th Street. Then turn west to reach 27th Street (S. Layton Boulevard). Travel south on 27th Street to reach the park.
Facilities: Picnic tables, toilets, baseball, tennis, playground.

O'Donnell Park

This park has a structured downtown setting, but it does offer scenic views of Lake Michigan, particularly from the two major pavilions in the park. The Miller Brewing Company Pavilion on the lakefront is available for rent. Visitors can also visit the Pavilion Restaurant or the Betty Brinn Children's Museum, which has hands-on displays and performances. Located near the Summerfest grounds, the park contains a bike trail and free concerts on Wednesdays.

Directions: In Milwaukee, take I-94 east to Lake Drive.
Facilities: Picnic tables, toilets, playground.

South Shore Park

Featuring a sand beach on Lake Michigan, this park also takes advantage of its lake access with a boat launch, a pavilion overlooking the lake, and fishing access, which is complemented by a fish-cleaning station. The park also offers sand volleyball, a playground and two horseshoe pits.

Directions: In Milwaukee, take I-94 to I-794. Continue to the end and bear to the right at the Port of Milwaukee. Turn off the freeway and make a left toward the bay. Then turn right and follow the road to Superior. Turn left onto Superior and follow it to the park.

Facilities: Picnic tables, toilets, swimming, beach, volleyball, playground, boat landing.

Veterans Park

Dedicated to veterans, this 92-acre park features a Vietnam Memorial. It also offers fishing in Juneau Lagoon, a rugby field, bike and in-line skate rentals, a 20-stop exercise course, a three-mile jogging trail and access to the "76" bike trail.

Directions: In Milwaukee, take I-94 (794) east to Lincoln Memorial Drive. Travel north on Lincoln Memorial.

Facilities: Picnic tables, toilets, playground.

Fish from the pier or from your boat, or simply enjoy the lake view, at Timm's Hill Park in Price County.

Warnimont Park

This site features an 18-hole, par 3 golf course, which includes night golf and a restaurant. The park also offers an archery range, an in-line skate hockey court, fitness trails and a senior center. Dogs are not allowed.

Directions: In Milwaukee, take I-94 to I-794. Continue to the end and bear to the right at the Port of Milwaukee. Turn off the freeway and make a left toward the bay. Then turn right and follow the road to Superior. Turn left onto Superior, which later turns into S. Lake Drive, and follow it a few miles to the park.

Facilities: Picnic tables, toilets, golf, playground.

Whitnall Park

At 640 acres, this park is the largest and most complete in the county system. It features Boerner Botanical Gardens, home to the Rose Festival in June. This large facility includes gardens and walkways, along with a Garden House and exhibit rooms. The facility, which hosts summer concerts, can be rented for special occasions. The park also contains the Wehr Nature Center, an environmental education facility with a network of more than five miles of nature trails. These trails also provide access to the wetland boardwalk, a study area in the woodlands, and Mallard Lake, which has a bird observation shelter and a waterfall. The visitor center contains exhibits and an outdoor amphitheater and offers programs. The park includes three designated picnic areas, an archery range, a cross-country ski trail, toboggan slides and an 18-hole golf course with championship layout; golf lessons and a restaurant are available. On Fridays, visitors can enjoy free summer movies or a fish fry. Visitors can also rent an overnight lodge that sleeps 21 and has a fireplace and kitchen.

> **Directions:** In Milwaukee, take I-94 east to Highway 45. Turn south to the interchange with I-43. Take I-43 west until you can rejoin with Highway 45, then continue to travel south on Highway 45. The park entrance is just south of Forest Home Avenue on Highway 45.
>
> **Facilities:** Picnic tables, toilets, hiking, nature trails, cross-country skiing, golf, playground.

Wilson Park

Directly adjacent to Wilson Recreational Area, this 78-acre site features a lagoon offering ice skating and fishing. A pavilion is available for rent. Visitors can also enjoy five picnic areas, a swimming pool, a baseball diamond and a senior center.

> **Directions:** In Milwaukee, take Highway 45 south to Oklahoma Avenue exit. Turn east and travel to Highway 41. Turn south and continue to Howard Avenue. Turn east and continue to the park.
>
> **Facilities:** Picnic tables, toilets, swimming, baseball, playground.

Wilson Recreational Area

This 58-acre site, directly adjacent to Wilson Park, contains a picnic area, a pavilion, a senior center, an ice skating rink, concessions, three tennis courts, a basketball court, a soccer field and sand volleyball.

Directions: In Milwaukee, take Highway 45 south to the Oklahoma Avenue exit. Turn east and travel to Highway 41. Turn south and continue to Howard Avenue. Turn east and continue to the park.

Facilities: Picnic tables, toilets, baseball, volleyball, tennis, playground.

MONROE COUNTY

Contact: Monroe County Park Department
Rt. 2, Box 21A
Sparta, WI 54656
(608) 269-8738

McMullen Park

Situated on 600 acres of Monroe County forest land, McMullen Park contains 30 campsites, hiking and nearby hunting in a wilderness setting. Lake Wazeda, a 30-acre cranberry flowage, hosts populations of pan fish, largemouth bass, northern pike and bullhead. The hiking trails lead up a 150-foot bluff for a panoramic view of three counties.

Directions: Take Highway 12 to Abbey Lane in Warrens and turn east. Follow Abbey Lane to 24th Avenue.

Facilities: Picnic tables, picnic shelter, outhouses, tent sites, hiking, nature trails, playground, boat landing.

OCONTO COUNTY

Contact: Oconto County Forestry and Parks
Courthouse
301 Washington St.
Oconto, WI 54153
(414) 834-6827

Chute Pond Park

Located on the Oconto River Flowage, Chute Pond County Park features waterfalls visible from one of the hiking trails in the park. Visitors can also take advantage of the water access by renting a boat or swimming from a grass beach. Picnic tables and campsites are available.

Directions: From Mountain, travel south on Highway 32 to East Shore Drive. Turn west and continue to the park.

Facilities: Picnic tables, outhouses, tent sites, trailer sites, swimming, beach, hiking, boat landing.

County Park 1

This park contains a boat landing providing access to Green Bay.
    Directions: From Oconto, take Highway 41 north 3½ miles to County A. Turn east and go two miles to County Y. Turn north and go 2½ miles to the landing.
    Facilities: Boat landing only.

Gillett Park

This small park on the Oconto River offers a place for fishing and boat portaging.
    Directions: From Gillett, take County BB south 2¼ miles to the river.
    Facilities: Boat landing only.

Grange Park

Mainly a day-use park, Grange park provides a spot for picnicking and fishing on Little River.
    Directions: From Oconto, take Highway 41 north four miles to County A. Turn west and travel five miles. Cross Little River to the park.
    Facilities: Picnic shelter, outhouses.

Machickanee Public Boat Access

With access to the Machickanee Flowage of the Oconto River, the park provides entry for fishing and boating. Anglers can hook northern pike, walleye, large and smallmouth bass, pan fish, trout and salmon. The boat landing provides access for good canoeing, waterskiing and recreational boating.
    Directions: From Oconto Falls, take Highway 22 east to Highway 141. Turn south and travel 2½ miles to Chicken Shack Road. Turn west and go to Landing Lane. Continue west to the park.
    Facilities: Outhouses, boat landing.

North Bay Shore Recreation Area

A good spot for perch and salmon fishing, this park provides boating access to Green Bay. Picnic tables are set up throughout the park, and a shelter can be rented. There is also a playground, along with areas for volleyball, basketball and horseshoes. Thirty-three campsites are available.
    Directions: From Oconto, take Highway 41 north 3½ miles to County A. Turn east and travel two miles to County Y. Turn north and travel 3½ miles to the park.

Facilities: Picnic tables, picnic shelter, outhouses, tent sites, trailer sites, volleyball, playground, boat landing.

Patzer Park

This small park on the Oconto River provides a spot for boating and picnicking.
Directions: From Gillett, take Highway 32 north about one mile to County H. Turn west and travel about five miles to Hintz. The park will be on the southwest side of the Oconto River in town.
Facilities: Picnic tables, outhouses, boat landing.

Pioneer Park

Situated on 80 acres of majestic pines, Pioneer Park offers a fishing pond primarily for day use.
Directions: From Oconto Falls, take Highway 22 east to Highway 141. Travel south about 1½ miles to County I, just north of the Oconto River. Turn west and go ⅛ mile to Pioneer Park Road. Turn north and travel ½ mile to the park.
Facilities: None.

ONEIDA COUNTY

Contact: Oneida County Forestry Department
P.O. Box 400
Rhinelander, WI 54501
(715) 369-6140

Almon Recreation Area

Just four miles south of Rhinelander, Almon Recreation Area offers an extensive system of hiking and nature trails. Swimmers and beach-goers have to walk through the woods to get to the sand beach on Buck Lake. Picnic facilities are also provided.
Directions: From Rhinelander, take County G southeast two miles to Laffig Road. Go south on Laffig Road a half mile to Hixon Lake Road and turn west (right). The park entrance is about a mile down the road.
Facilities: Picnic tables, picnic shelter, outhouses, swimming, beach, dressing rooms, hiking, nature trails.

Bass Lake Park

As its name suggests, Bass Lake is a fishing lake, stocked with northern pike, bass and pan fish. The park offers a rustic picnic area and boat landing.

Directions: Go west from Rhinelander on Highway 8 about 25 miles to McCord Road. Go north five miles on McCord Road to Bass Lake Road. Go east on Bass Lake Road to the park entrance.
Facilities: Picnic tables, outhouses, boat landing.

Perch Lake Park

Anglers will appreciate Perch Lake for the trout that are planted here each year. The park provides picnic tables and a boat landing for nonmotorized boats.
Directions: Take County K eight miles west of Rhinelander to Washburn Lake Road and go south. Turn east on Trout Creek Road, and go ¼ mile to the entrance.
Facilities: Picnic tables, outhouses, boat landing.

Town Line Lake Park

Despite its location only two miles from Rhinelander, Town Line Lake Park has an out-of-the-way environment. Picnickers, beach-goers and hikers will enjoy the scenic view of Town Line Lake. The park also provides a boat launch.
Directions: From Rhinelander, take County K west ¼ mile to the park.
Facilities: Picnic tables, picnic shelter, outhouses, swimming, beach, hiking, playground, boat landing.

OUTAGAMIE COUNTY

Contact: Outagamie County Parks Department
1375 E. Broadway Drive
Appleton, WI 54915
(414) 832-4791

Barker Park

The Wolf River is popular with powerboating enthusiasts and anglers in search of walleye, bass, northern pike or catfish. Canoeing is difficult on this river. Barker Park, in addition to its boat landing, provides a picnic area.
Directions: From New London, take Highway 45 north to Highway 54. Turn east on Highway 54 and travel about eight miles to Old 54 Road. Turn south and continue to the park.
Facilities: Picnic tables, boat landing.

Black Otter Park

Located in the south corner of Hortonville, this park offers a view of Black Otter Lake, picnic facilities and a boat landing.

Directions: From New London, take Highway 45 east to Hortonville.
Facilities: Picnic tables, picnic shelter, boat landing.

Buchman Access

This roadside park offers a boat landing and picnic spot on the Wolf River.
Directions: From New London, take Highway 45 east to Hortonville. Then turn
north on County M and continue to the park.
Facilities: Picnic tables, boat landing.

Koepke Access

A boat landing in this park provides access to the Wolf River. There is also a picnic
area on the site.
Directions: From New London, take Highway 45 north to Highway 54. Turn
east on Highway 54 and travel about eight miles to Highway 76. Turn north
and go about 1½ miles to Koepke Road. Turn west and continue to the access.
Facilities: Picnic tables, boat landing.

Mosquito Hill Nature Center

An extensive network of hiking trails winds through this 430-acre interpretive
nature preserve just east of New London. Open to the public Saturdays and
Sundays, Mosquito Hill Nature Center offers a full schedule of guided hikes
and nature programs. Snowshoes may be rented in the winter.
Directions: From New London, travel east on County S.
Facilities: Toilets, hiking, nature trails.

Plamann Park

Plamann County Park, located north of Appleton, is a popular outdoor
recreation spot year-round. Summer activities include swimming and sunbathing
on the beach at manmade Lake Plamann, hiking the nature trails, visiting the
small farm of baby animals, and playing baseball, volleyball, tennis and disc golf.
In the winter, park users ice skate, toboggan, snowmobile, and cross-country ski.
Directions: From Appleton, take Highway 47 north to Broadway Drive. Turn
east and continue to the park.
Facilities: Picnic tables, picnic shelters, toilets, swimming, beach, dressing
rooms, hiking, nature trails, cross-country skiing, baseball, volleyball, tennis,
playground.

Stephensville Access

Stephensville Access is a boat landing on the Wolf River, primarily used by
powerboats.
Directions: From New London, take County S east about seven miles.
Facilities: Picnic tables, boat landing.

OZAUKEE COUNTY

Contact: Ozaukee County Park Commission
121 W. Main St.
P.O. Box 994
Port Washington, WI 53074-0994
(414) 284-8258

Carlson Park

The Ozaukee Ice Center, with indoor and outdoor ice skating rinks, is located at Carlson Park in Mequon.
> **Directions:** Take Highway 57 through Mequon north to Pioneer Road. Go east on Pioneer Road to the park.
> **Facilities:** Toilets.

Covered Bridge Park

The "Red Bridge," built in 1867, stands in Covered Bridge Park as the last of more than 40 covered bridges that once stood in Wisconsin. The 12-acre park offers scenic picnicking and fishing on Cedar Creek. Grills are located throughout the park.
> **Directions:** Take Highway 143 north from Cedarburg to its intersection with Highway 60 and Covered Bridge Road. Follow Covered Bridge Road to the park.
> **Facilities:** Picnic tables, outhouses.

Ehlers Park

This small wayside park on the Milwaukee River is a scenic spot for picnicking and fishing .
> **Directions:** Take Highway 33 in Saukville to County W. Go north on County W to the park.
> **Facilities:** Picnic tables.

Hawthorne Hills Park

This park features an 18-hole golf course and clubhouse, picnic areas and a nature trail through the woods. During the winter months, activities include sledding and cross-country skiing on the golf course (trails are not groomed). The historic Pioneer Village, a group of restored buildings including a barn, train station and a farmhouse, is located on the north edge of the park.
> **Directions:** Take Highway 33 northwest of Saukville to County I. Go north on County I three miles to the park.
> **Facilities:** Picnic tables, hiking, nature trails, cross-country skiing, golf.

Mee-Kwon Park Golf Course

Visitors can play 18 holes of golf, fish in the park's lagoon, picnic, or take a walk on the short nature trail. In the winter, the park offers a pond for ice skating, a sledding hill and cross-country skiing on the golf course.

Directions: Take I-43 to Mequon Road and go west. Go north at Highway 57 and follow it to Bonniwell Road.

Facilities: Picnic tables, toilets, cross-country skiing, baseball, golf.

Virmond Park

Virmond Park's location on the bluffs of Lake Michigan makes for a pleasant picnic. A shelter, tables and grills are provided. A portion of the park's 66 acres is left undisturbed as a nature preserve. Other facilities include soccer fields, tennis courts and two baseball fields.

Directions: Take I-43 to Mequon Road and go east. Go south on Lake Shore Road to the park.

Facilities: Picnic tables, picnic shelter, toilets, baseball, volleyball, tennis, playground.

Waubedonia Park

Waubedonia Park is a quiet spot to camp, fish, and picnic along the Milwaukee River. Six campsites and canoe access to the river are available. The park also has tennis courts, baseball fields and grills.

Directions: Take Highway 57 to County H in Fredonia.

Facilities: Picnic tables, outhouses, tent sites, trailer sites, baseball, tennis, playground, canoe landing.

PEPIN COUNTY

Contact: Pepin County Parks
P.O. Box 39
Durand, WI 54736
(715) 672-8665

Holden Park

Primarily used for picnics and rugged camping, Holden Park has 18 campsites with electricity, a small wildlife area and a rifle range. The park adjoins Silver Birch Lake Park, which provides access to Silver Birch Lake for fishing, swimming and small boats. There is also a handicapped-accessible fishing pier.

Directions: From Durand, take Highway 10 northwest to County N. Go west on County N four or five miles to County NN. Turn left and follow the road to the park.

Facilities: Picnic tables, outhouses, tent sites.

PIERCE COUNTY

Contact: Nugget Lake County Park
RR 1, Box 213B
Plum City, WI 54761
(715) 639-5611

Nugget Lake Park

Within Nugget Lake County Park's 752 acres of semiwilderness, outdoor enthusiasts will find plenty to keep them occupied. Year-round, anglers may hook largemouth bass, bluegill, pumpkinseed, black crappie and walleye in 116-acre Nugget Lake. Canoes and boats can be rented by the hour, and a sandy shoreline provides a spot to sun and swim. The campground has 55 campsites (some with electricity) and hot showers. More than six miles of hiking trails, with benches and scenic overlooks along the way, double as cross-country ski trails in the winter. An outdoor amphitheater shows nature films on summer weekends.

    Directions: From Ellsworth, take Highway 10 east past the Rush River to County CC. Go north three miles on County CC to County HH. Go east two miles to the park.

    Facilities: Picnic tables, picnic shelter, outhouses, toilets, tent sites, trailer sites, swimming, beach, dressing rooms, hiking, nature trails, cross-country skiing, playground, boat landing.

POLK COUNTY

Contact: Polk County Parks
100 Polk County Plaza
Balsam Lake, WI 54810
(715) 485-9294

Apple River Park

Located on the shores of the Apple River, this 18-acre park offers a picnic spot and hiking trails. The Apple River is fairly fast and runs too shallow for most boats except canoes.

Directions: From Highway 8, take County H south one mile to Mains Crossing Avenue. Turn east and go one mile to the park.

Facilities: Picnic tables, picnic shelter, outhouses, hiking, nature trails, playground, canoe landing.

Atlas Park

Atlas Park is comprised of three areas separated by the waters of Long Trade Lake and Long Trade River, and connected by walkways. The lake, to which anglers have boat access, has populations of bass, northern pike and pan fish. Several picnic areas, a baseball diamond and a walking trail that circles the park offer visitors additional recreational opportunities.

Directions: From Highway 35 just north of Luck, turn west onto County B. Continue eight miles to the park.

Facilities: Picnic tables, picnic shelter, outhouses, hiking, baseball, playground, boat landing.

Black Brook Park

Anglers can fish above and below the Black Brook Dam on the Apple River for muskellunge and northern pike. Icefishers are likely to find perch, pan fish and northern pike. The park provides several picnic areas and canoe access to the river.

Directions: From the junction of County A and Highway 46, take Highway 46 north to County CC. Continue north on County CC two miles to 40th Avenue. Turn west and go ½ mile to the park.

Facilities: Picnic tables, outhouses, playground, canoe landing.

Kennedy Environmental Area

A 1½-mile trail, handicapped accessible, meanders through this natural area and across the Balsam Branch Stream. April brings visitors to see the spring spawn run of muskellunge, northern pike and walleye from the viewing dock. Schools frequently use Kennedy Environmental Area for outdoor recreation and nature study.

Directions: From the junction of Highway 65 and Highway 8, take Highway 8 east to 150th Street. Turn south and go one mile to 120th Avenue. Turn east and go ½ mile to Kennedy Mill Avenue. Turn south and go ¼ mile.

Facilities: Picnic tables, outhouses, nature trails.

Lotus Lake Park

The northernmost beds of American lotus in the state float on Lotus Lake. Visitors get a chance to see the flowery plants along the looped nature trail, which winds through the woods. The park also provides picnic areas and a boat landing.

Directions: From the junction of Highway 35 and County M in Osceola, take County M east four miles to County MM. Go north two miles to 90th Avenue. Turn east and travel one mile.

Facilities: Picnic tables, picnic shelter, outhouses, hiking, nature trails, playground, boat landing.

Somers Lake Recreation Area

This 139-acre area has three miles of hiking and cross-country ski trails, and is open to hunting and fishing on Somers Lake.

Directions: From Frederic, take Highway 35 south to County W. Turn east and travel five miles to County I. Turn north and go one mile to the access road.

Facilities: Hiking, cross-country skiing.

PORTAGE COUNTY

Contact: Portage County Parks
County-City Building
1516 Church St.
Stevens Point, WI 54481
(715) 346-1433

Becker Lake Recreation Area

A 40-acre undeveloped lake, also called Baker Lake. This is a public hunting area.

Directions: From Stevens Point, take Highway 66 northeast about six miles to Ellis. Turn north on Ellis Road and travel two miles.

Facilities: None.

Cate Park

This remote park on the Tomorrow River, which is a small stream, offers a spot for children to fish. It has one picnic table and receives very little use.

Directions: From Stevens Point, take Highway 10 southeast to Amherst. In Amherst, turn northeast on School Road and go ½ mile.

Facilities: Picnic table, outhouses, boat landing.

Collins Park

Forty-two acre Collins Lake is good for swimming and for fishing for northern pike, walleye, bass and pan fish. The park, which has 27 wooded campsites, is less developed than the county's other campgrounds. There is a small beach and a playground.

Directions: From Stevens Point, take Highway 66 northeast about 13 miles to County I, about two miles west of Rosholt. Turn south on County I and continue to the park.

Facilities: Picnic tables, picnic shelter, outhouses, tent sites, trailer sites, swimming, beach, dressing rooms, playground, boat landing.

Consolidated Park

This strip of land along the Wisconsin River is commonly used for shore fishing and boat access to the river. The park, located on the west side of Stevens Point, also has picnic tables.

Directions: The park is located in Stevens Point on West River Drive.

Facilities: Picnic tables, outhouses, boat landing.

Dewey Shooting Range

Within the limits of its 319 acres, visitors can shoot handguns, shotguns and rifles at the 25-, 50-, 100- and 200-yard public ranges. Ear muffs, spotting scopes and sand bags may be rented. The Dewey Shooting Range is also part of a 5,000-acre public hunting area.

Directions: From Stevens Point, take Highway 66 northeast about three miles to County Y. Turn north and travel 2½ miles to Dewey Drive. Turn west and travel another 2½ miles to Willow Spring Drive. Turn north and continue to the range.

Facilities: Toilets.

DuBay Park

Its location on 600-acre Lake DuBay makes DuBay Park a popular spot for water activity—fishing, sailing, waterskiing, jetskiing and swimming. Thirty-one campsites are available, all wooded and equipped with electricity. The park also offers a sand beach, playground, baseball field and picnic facilities.

Directions: From Stevens Point, take Highway 10 northeast to Highway 34. Turn north on 34 and travel 5½ miles to County E. Turn east on County E and continue to the park, which is about one mile south of Dancy.

Facilities: Picnic tables, picnic shelter, outhouses, tent sites, trailer sites, swimming, beach, baseball, playground, boat landing.

Frost Park

Area residents often picnic at Frost Park, just northwest of Almond. The park has picnic tables, a shelter and fireplaces.

Directions: From the junction of Highway 51 and County W near Bancroft, take County W east through Bancroft to County BB. Turn south on BB and continue to the park.

Facilities: Picnic tables, picnic shelter, outhouses.

Galecke Park

Boaters, anglers and waterskiiers extensively use Galecke Park, located along the Wisconsin River west of Plover. Picnic facilities, including a shelter and fireplaces, are also provided.

Directions: From Plover, take River Drive west 1½ miles.

Facilities: Picnic tables, picnic shelter, outhouses, boat landing.

Jordan Park

Jordan Park is set up for outdoor education with its nature center, extensive system of nature and hiking trails, and deer pen. The park offers 22 campsites, all with electricity except for three canoe sites on the Plover River. A handicapped-accessible site can also be reserved. The Jordan Pond, an 85-acre body of water with northern pike, bass and pan fish, borders the park, providing opportunities to swim, boat, fish and sunbath on the beach. Three cross-country ski trails provide winter recreation.

Directions: From Stevens Point, take Highway 66 northeast three miles to the park.

Facilities: Picnic tables, picnic shelter, outhouses, tent sites, trailer sites, swimming, beach, hiking, nature trails, cross-country skiing, baseball, volleyball, playground, boat landing.

Lake Emily Park

The most heavily used park in Portage County, Lake Emily Park offers 49 campsites, complete with electricity and showers, in a pine plantation forest. Lake Emily covers 96 acres and draws swimmers, beach-goers, boaters and waterskiers. Anglers will find northern pike, walleye, bass and pan fish. The park also has a hiking trail, a pen with deer and turkeys, and, in winter, cross-country ski trails.

Directions: From Stevens Point, take Highway 10 southeast to Amherst Junction.

Facilities: Picnic tables, picnic shelter, outhouses, toilets, tent sites, trailer sites, swimming, beach, dressing rooms, hiking, cross-country skiing, baseball, playground, boat landing.

Lake Helen Park

Lake Helen Park is a day-use park just east of Rosholt, with a swimming beach, playground, boat landing and picnic facilities with fireplaces. Anglers on 87-acre Lake Helen will find northern pike, walleye, bass and pan fish.

Directions: From Stevens Point, take Highway 66 east through Rosholt. Continue 3½ miles east on 66 to Lake Helen Road. Turn south and continue to the park.

Facilities: Picnic tables, outhouses, swimming, beach, playground, boat landing.

Meyers Lake

Boat landing on 27-acre Meyers Lake, where anglers will find northern pike, bass and pan fish.

Directions: From Stevens Point, take Highway 10 southeast to Amherst. In Amherst, turn north on County A and travel two miles to Lake Meyers Road. Turn west and continue to the landing.

Facilities: Boat landing only.

Peterson Park

Visitors to Peterson Park can swim, boat, waterski and fish on 74-acre Tree Lake, just north of Rosholt. This day-use park also offers picnic tables, fireplaces and a playground.

Directions: From Stevens Point, take Highway 66 east 1½ miles past Rosholt. Turn north on Highway 49 and go three miles to Tree Lake Road. Turn west and continue to the park.

Facilities: Picnic tables, outhouses, swimming, beach, playground, boat landing.

Plover River Wayside

Canoeists can launch their boat into the Plover River here, at this wayside on Highway 51 just south of Plover. Picnic tables and fireplaces are also provided.

Directions: From Stevens Point, take Highway 66 east to County Y. Turn north and travel 3½ miles to County K. Turn east and continue to Plover River.

Facilities: Picnic tables, boat landing.

Rinehart Lake

Boat landing on 43-acre Rinehart Lake, where anglers will find northern pike, bass and pan fish.

Directions: From Stevens Point, take Highway 10 southeast to its junction with Highway 161 in Amherst Junction. Take 161 north through Nelsonville, then continue east on Highway 161 to County T. Turn north and go one mile to South Lake Road. Turn west and continue to the landing.

Facilities: Boat landing only.

Standing Rocks Park

During the winter months, Standing Rocks Park offers five downhill ski runs, groomed cross-country ski trails and a ski lodge in which skiers can warm up and relax. When the snow melts, visitors can hike, mountain bike and picnic near Bear Lake.

Directions: From Plover, take County B east five miles to Custer Road. Turn south and travel 1¼ miles to Standing Rocks Road. Turn east and continue to the park.
Facilities: Picnic tables, outhouses, toilets, hiking, cross-country skiing.

Stedman Park

An old highway right of way, Stedman Park now provides a few picnic tables and a spot to fish on the scenic but small Waupaca River.
Directions: From Plover, take Highway 54 southeast approximately 18 miles to County D. Turn north and travel two miles to the park.
Facilities: Picnic tables.

Sunset Lake Park

People travel from a 50-mile radius to swim and sun at this park's beach, the largest in the county. Sunset Lake, 63 acres, also offers opportunities to boat and fish for bass, pan fish and trout. Other facilities include picnic tables, fireplaces and a playground.
Directions: From Stevens Point, take Highway 10 southeast to its junction with Highway 161 in Amherst Junction. Take Highway 161 north through Nelson-ville, then continue east one mile on Highway 161 to County A. Turn north and travel 2½ miles to County MM. Turn east and go one mile to Sunset Lake Road. Turn north and continue to the park.
Facilities: Picnic tables, outhouses, swimming, beach, playground, boat landing.

Tech Park

Tech Park is adjacent to Consolidated Park, and provides a spot to fish and picnic on the Wisconsin River. Fireplaces are available.
Directions: Located in Stevens Point on West River Drive.
Facilities: Picnic tables.

Tomorrow River Wayside

Anglers have access to the Tomorrow River at this site just northwest of Nelsonville.
Directions: From Stevens Point, take Highway 10 southeast to its junction with Highway 161 in Amherst Junction. Take Highway 161 north to Nelsonville. Turn northwest on County Q and continue 1½ miles to the wayside.
Facilities: None.

Wisconsin River Recreation Area

Located 10 miles north of Stevens Point, this park provides fishing access to the Wisconsin River and also serves as a public hunting area.

Directions: From Stevens Point, take Highway 51 north about nine miles to County DB. Turn west and go ½ mile to River Road. Turn south and travel one mile to the park.

Facilities: None.

Wolf Lake Park

This remote park receives little use, but has a large swimming beach and a boat landing on 36-acre Wolf Lake. Anglers will find walleye, bass and pan fish. Other than the park, there is no development on the lake, which makes for quiet picnics and hikes and, in winter, secluded cross-country skiing.

Directions: From the southern county line, take Highway 51 north to County D. Turn east and continue to Almond. In Almond, turn north on County A and travel two miles to County EE. Turn north and go three miles to County GG. Turn east and continue two miles to Wolf Lake Road. Turn south and continue to the park.

Facilities: Picnic tables, outhouses, swimming, beach, hiking, cross-country skiing, boat landing.

PRICE COUNTY

Contact: Price County Tourism
Price County Courthouse
126 Cherry St.
Phillips, WI 54555
(800) 269-4505, (715) 339-4505

Big Falls Park

Located on the south fork of the Jump River, Big Falls County Park offers primitive, rustic camping and a good spot to fish for walleye, muskellunge and bass. White and red pine trees, and an occasional glimpse of white-tailed deer and bald eagles, make this park both picturesque and peaceful.

Directions: From Phillips, go three miles south on Highway 13. Take Highway 111 five miles southwest.

Facilities: Picnic tables, picnic shelter, outhouses, tent sites, hiking, playground, volleyball.

Solberg Lake Park

Located just northwest of Phillips on Solberg Lake, Solberg Lake County Park has a 45-site campground, swimming beach, picnic areas and a boat landing. Some of the campsites are on the lake; all have electricity and access to showers. The park also has a short nature trail, but hikers can cross the street for more extensive trails.

> **Directions:** From Phillips, take Highway 13 to Old 13 Road. Follow Old 13 to West Solberg Road and go east to the park.
>
> **Facilities:** Picnic tables, picnic shelter, outhouses, toilets, tent sites, trailer sites, swimming, beach, hiking, nature trails, volleyball, playground, boat landing.

Timm's Hill Park

Originally settled as a logging camp, Timm's Hill County Park offers outdoor recreation and scenic views from Timm's Hill, the highest geographic point in Wisconsin. Looped hiking trails wind through woods and around spring-fed Timm's Lake and Bass Lake. Anglers can fish from pier or boat on either lake, and will likely find bass and pan fish. Other opportunities include cross-country skiing the park's seven and a half miles of groomed trails, biking on the Ice Age Trail, using adjacent snowmobile trails, and climbing the 50-foot observation tower for a bird's-eye view of the landscape.

> **Directions:** From Ogema, go east on Highway 86 to County C. Go south on County C to Rustic Road and go east to the park.
>
> **Facilities:** Picnic tables, picnic shelter, outhouses, hiking, cross-country skiing, playground, boat landing.

Wisconsin Concrete Park

This unique park exhibits more than 200 of Fred Smith's eclectic sculptures. Once dubbed the "Picasso of the Northwoods," Smith, a former farmer, lumberjack and tavern-owner, began sculpting as a hobby at age 65. Smith forged unconventional materials, such as mirrors, metal and cement, into figures of Paul Bunyan, Kit Carson and his wild stallion, Abe Lincoln and even the Statue of Liberty.

> **Directions:** Take Highway 13 south of Phillips.
>
> **Facilities:** Outhouses, nature trails.

RACINE COUNTY

Contact: Racine County Public Works/Parks Department
14200 Washington Ave.
Sturtevant, WI 53177-1253
(414) 886-8440

Beaumont Park

Beaumont Park is a picnic wayside with tables, grills and access to snowmobile trails.

Directions: From Racine, take Highway 20 west 16 miles to the junction with Highway 75 and County S.

Facilities: Picnic tables, outhouses.

Brown's Lake Golf Course

The Lower Fox River flows through this 18-hole regulation golf course, located on Brown's Lake. Brown's Lake Golf Course also provides a practice golf range and putting green, and three lighted tennis courts. In the winter, a three-mile cross-country ski trail winds through and around the course.

Directions: From Burlington, take Highway 11 east to County W. Turn north and travel 7/10 mile.

Facilities: Outhouses, toilets, cross-country skiing, tennis, golf.

Bushnell Park

Bushnell Park, located just south of Burlington, features a soccer field, two lighted baseball diamonds, nine competition horseshoe pitching courts and a hiking trail. The park sits on the lower Fox River, which provides opportunities to shore fish and launch a canoe. The picnic shelter has a large open fire hearth, tables and grills.

Directions: From the junction of Highway 11 and Highway 142 in Burlington, take Highway 142 southeast ½ mile.

Facilities: Picnic tables, picnic shelter, outhouses, toilets, hiking, baseball, playground.

Cliffside Park

Situated high above the shoreline of Lake Michigan, Cliffside Park offers a wide variety of outdoor athletic facilities—four baseball diamonds, four tennis courts, two basketball courts, two soccer fields and a nature trail that winds through a wooded ravine. The park has a 92-site campground with three large group sites, electricity and showers.

Directions: From Racine, take Highway 32 north four miles to Seven Mile Road. Turn east and go to Michna Road. Travel south ½ mile.

Facilities: Picnic tables, toilets, tent sites, trailer sites, hiking, nature trails, baseball, tennis, playground.

Colonel Heg Memorial Park

A museum at Colonel Heg Memorial Park highlights the heritage of the early Norwegian settlers who made western Racine County their "New Norway." The park also offers picnic areas with shelters and grills, a baseball diamond, and horseshoe pitching courts.

Directions: From Waterford, take Loomis Road north to Heg Park Road.

Facilities: Picnic tables, picnic shelter, toilets, baseball, playground.

Eagle Lake Park

Anglers will appreciate Eagle Lake, stocked with just about every native freshwater fish. Eagle Lake Park provides a boat launch, a fishing pier and room along the banks for casting a line. Visitors can also picnic, play baseball or pitch horseshoes.

Directions: From Burlington, take Highway 11 east eight miles to Sunnyside Drive. Turn north and go to Church Road. Turn east and continue to the park.

Facilities: Picnic tables, picnic shelter, toilets, baseball, playground, boat landing.

Ela Property

Several small ponds and the waters of the Fox River make this park a good spot for shore fishing. Ela Property's 239 acres are otherwise undeveloped, except for several nature trails. Winter visitors can access snowmobile trails here.

Directions: From Waterford, take Highway 20 south to Highway 36. Turn south on 36 and continue to the junction with County J, just south of Rochester.

Facilities: Nature trails.

Evans Park

This wooded area, equipped with tables and grills, is used primarily as a picnic spot. An unmarked hiking trail runs through the park.

Directions: From Racine, take Highway 20 west 10 miles to the park, ¼ mile west of I-94.

Facilities: Picnic tables, outhouses, hiking.

Fischer Park

Fischer Park, on the southeast shore of Brown's Lake, has a large sand beach, a beachhouse and concessions. On Saturday evenings, the Aqueducts, a local water-ski show, performs on the lake. The park also provides picnic tables and grills, a softball diamond and a boat launch.

Directions: From Burlington, take Highway 11 east two miles.

Facilities: Picnic tables, toilets, swimming, beach, baseball, boat landing.

Ives Grove Golf Links

This county-owned, privately operated 18-hole golf course features watered bentgrass greens, tees and fairways, two practice putting greens and a practice golf range. An air-conditioned clubhouse has a restaurant, golf shop and showers. In the winter, a two-mile cross-country ski trail leads skiers around the entire course.

Directions: From Racine, take Highway 20 west 10 miles to the park, ¼ mile west of I-94.

Facilities: Outhouses, toilets, cross-country skiing, golf.

John Margis Jr. Wildlife Area

An elevated boardwalk extends through this 45-acre wildlife area, connecting to a marsh and two of the three ponds. A former state fish hatchery, the site features a nature trail overlooking the largest pond. A creek trickles off the adjacent Bohner's Lake. Visitors may catch a glimpse of waterfowl while enjoying a picnic on the grounds.

Directions: From Burlington, take County P south three miles to Fish Hatchery Road. Travel ½ mile southeast on Fish Hatchery Road to the wildlife area.

Facilities: Picnic tables, hiking, nature trails.

Koerber Property

A tributary of the Root River runs through the 11-acre Koerber Property, used primarily as a wayside picnic area. Visitors have access to snowmobile trails and a baseball diamond.

Directions: From Milwaukee, take I-94 south to County G in Kilbournville. Turn west and travel two miles.

Facilities: Outhouses, baseball.

Old Settlers' Park

Old Settlers' Park, located next to the Racine County fairgrounds, offers eight reservable picnic areas, six shelters with electricity, picnic tables and grills. The park is used for conducting the annual Racine County Fair.

Directions: From the junction of Highway 45 and Highway 11 in Union Grove, take Highway 11 west ½ mile.

Facilities: Picnic tables, picnic shelter, toilets, baseball, playground.

Pritchard Park

Located just south of Racine, Pritchard Park offers a spot to picnic, play baseball or go for a jog. The picnic facilities include grills and one large shelter with electricity. Two baseball diamonds, a soccer field and a jogging trail are also provided.

Directions: In the city of Racine, take Ohio Street one block north of its junction with Highway 11.

Facilities: Picnic tables, picnic shelter, toilets, nature trails, baseball, playground.

Quarry Lake Park

The deep, clear, spring-fed waters of this former limestone quarry provide a place to swim, fish and scuba dive. The park has a multilevel, terraced sand beach and a floating dock system with diving boards and fishing piers. Eighteen-acre Quarry Lake is annually stocked with rainbow and brown trout. Other facilities include picnic areas with tables and grills, concessions and showers.

> **Directions:** From the junction of Highway 31 and Highway 38 just outside Racine, take Highway 38 one mile southeast.
> **Facilities:** Picnic tables, toilets, swimming, beach, dressing rooms, volleyball.

Racine Harbor Park

Anglers will appreciate the floating dock and breakwater at Racine Harbor Park, located in downtown Racine on Lake Michigan. The park also offers a fish-cleaning station and an elevated deck for a view of the harbor.

> **Directions:** In Racine, take Christopher Columbus Causeway 1½ blocks east of Main Street.
> **Facilities:** Toilets.

Root River Parkway Lands

Though it receives little use, this undeveloped piece of land along the Root River offers a spot to fish from the bank.

> **Directions:** Along the Root River near Caledonia; Horlick Dam location just east of Highway 38. Take Rapids Court one block west of the junction of North Green Bay Road and Rapids Drive.
> **Facilities:** None.

Saller Woods

Hiking and cross-country skiing trails wind through this quiet 91-acre site on the Fox River. A few picnic tables are provided.

> **Directions:** From Waterford, take Highway 20 southeast to Highway 36. Travel southwest on Highway 36 one mile south of Rochester to the Fox River.
> **Facilities:** Picnic tables, hiking, cross-country skiing.

Sanders Park

Visitors who take a walk along this park's nature trail through the 30-acre State Scientific Area will find more than 90 species of native wildflowers and a small creek flowing through an undisturbed forest floor. Sanders Park offers 39 campsites, four group sites and showers. There are six different picnic areas to choose from, equipped with tables and grills, and one large shelter with an open hearth fireplace. Other facilities include a baseball diamond, a soccer field, horseshoe pitching courts and a playground.

Directions: From Racine, take Highway 31 south to County KR. Turn east and go one mile to Wood Road. Turn north and travel ½ mile.

Facilities: Picnic tables, picnic shelter, toilets, tent sites, trailer sites, hiking, nature trails, baseball, playground.

Skewes Memorial Park

This four-acre wayside park, equipped with tables and grills, is a picnic spot and rest stop.

Directions: From Racine, take Highway 20 west one mile past I-94 to County C. Turn southwest and travel ½ mile.

Facilities: Picnic tables, outhouses.

Stenhouse-Babcock Park

Twelve acres of undeveloped land.

Directions: From Waterford, take Highway 20 southeast to Highway 36. Travel south on 36 to County J. Travel southeast on County J to the junction with County A.

Facilities: None.

Tabor Park

Tabor Park is a one-acre wayside picnic spot just north of Racine, equipped with tables and grills.

Directions: From Racine, take Highway 32 four miles north to the junction with Five Mile Road.

Facilities: Picnic tables.

W.R. Wadewitz Nature Camp

Formerly a Boy Scout camp, this natural resource area now serves as a primitive group camping site, offering a barn and three-sided Adirondack-style shelters and tent sites by reservation. Visitors can also hike and cross-country ski among some of the best glacial features and woodland vegetation in Racine County.

Directions: From the junction of Highway 20 and County W in Waterford, take County W 1½ miles south to Buena Park Road. Turn northwest and travel ¼ mile.

Facilities: Outhouses, hiking, nature trails, cross-country skiing.

RICHLAND COUNTY

Contact: Richland Center Chamber of Commerce
170 West Seminary
Richland Center, WI 53581
(608) 647-6205

Orion Boat Landing
This park on the Wisconsin River is used mainly as a boat launch.
Directions: From the intersection of Highway 80 and Highway 60 just north of Muscoda, take Highway 60 one mile east.
Facilities: Picnic tables, outhouses, boat landing.

Pier Park
The Pine River flows through a rock formation at Pier Park, creating a natural bridge. Visitors can take a short hike (¼ mile) up to the top of the rock for a great view of the area. The park offers open camping and picnic facilities.
Directions: From Richland Center, take Highway 80 north 10 miles to the community of Rockbridge.
Facilities: Picnic tables, picnic shelter, outhouses, tent sites, hiking, playground.

Port Andrews Park
Boat landing on the Wisconsin River.
Directions: From the intersection of Highway 80 and Highway 60 just north of Muscoda, take Highway 60 east six miles to the landing, near Blue River.
Facilities: Boat landing only.

Viola Park
This two-acre park offers a spot to picnic just east of Viola.
Directions: From Richland Center, take Highway 56 north 12 miles to the landing, which is one mile south of Viola.
Facilities: Picnic tables, picnic shelter, outhouses.

ROCK COUNTY

Contact: Rock County Department of Public Works
Parks Division
3715 Newville Road
Janesville, WI 53545
(608) 757-5450

Airport Park

Picnickers can watch the aircraft land and take off from the adjacent Rock County Airport. Tables and fireplaces are provided.

Directions: From Beloit, take Highway 51 north to its intersection with Knilans Road.

Facilities: Picnic tables.

Avon Park

Seventeen acres of undeveloped land on the Sugar River in Avon.

Directions: From Beloit, take Highway 81 west to West Beloit-Newark Road. Take this road west to its intersection with South Avon Store Road.

Facilities: None.

Beckman Mill Park

This 50-acre park contains the historic Beckman-Howe Mill, a 1920s grist mill. Visitors can picnic among the mixed oak woods, where tables and fireplaces are provided.

Directions: From Janesville, take Highway 11 west to County H. Go south on County H to West Mill Pond Road.

Facilities: Picnic tables, toilets.

Carver-Roehl Park

A scenic limestone outcropping stretches throughout 53-acre Carver-Roehl Park, located northeast of Clinton. Visitors can observe wildlife as they hike or cross-country ski the nature trails. Picnic tables and fireplaces are provided.

Directions: Take Highway 43 northeast from Clinton to South Carver's Rock Road. Go north on this road to the park.

Facilities: Picnic tables, outhouses, hiking, nature trails, cross-country skiing.

Emerald Grove Park

This 1.5-acre park in the Village of Emerald Grove offers a play area for children.

Directions: From Janesville, take County O east to Highway14-11 in Emerald Grove.

Facilities: Playground.

Gibbs Lake Park

At 299 acres, Gibbs Lake Park is Rock County's largest park, offering fishing and boating on Gibbs Lake, hiking and horseback riding in the summer, and cross-country skiing in the winter. The picnic area has tables and grills.

Directions: From Evansville, take Highway 14 east to North Eagle Road. Go north to West Gibbs Lake Road.

Facilities: Picnic tables, toilets, hiking, cross-country skiing, boat landing.

Happy Hollow Park

Happy Hollow River provides fishing and boating access to the Rock River. The park's 206 acres are largely undeveloped, except for a hiking trail and picnic tables.

Directions: From Janesville, go south on Highway 51 (Center Avenue) to Happy Hollow Road. Go west ¾ mile to the park.

Facilities: Picnic tables, outhouses, hiking, boat landing.

Ice Age Park

Three acres of undeveloped land in Harmony.

Directions: From Janesville, go north on I-90 to Kennedy Road. Take Kennedy Road north to Sable Drive.

Facilities: None.

Indianford Park

Located on a dam in the Rock River, Indianford Park is a good fishing spot.

Directions: From Janesville, take Highway 51 north to County F. Follow County F to its intersection with County M.

Facilities: Picnic tables, toilets.

Koshkonong Lake Access

Access for boating and fishing on Koshkonong Lake.

Directions: Take Highway 59 east of Edgerton to its intersection with Mallwood Road. Follow Mallwood Road to Hillside Drive, go north to Bay-view Drive, then turn left at Lakeside Drive.

Facilities: Boat access (no formal landing).

Lee Park

Forty-acre Lee County Park features a nature trail through a wooded area and into an arboretum, a small stream and a picnic area with a shelter and grills. Visitors can also use the softball diamond.

Directions: From Clinton, take Highway 140 south to its intersection with Highway 67.

Facilities: Picnic tables, picnic shelter, toilets, hiking, nature trails, baseball.

Magnolia Bluff Park

This 120-acre park west of Janesville features large rock outcroppings, vistas and bluffs. Visitors can take in the scenery by foot, cross-country ski, or horseback on several three-mile trails. A stand of white birch on the north face of Magnolia

Bluff provides a home for a variety of birds and wildlife. Picnic tables and grills are provided.

Directions: From Evansville, go south on Highway 213 three miles to Highway 59. Go west three and a half miles on Highway 59 to its intersection with Croak Road. Go south on Croak Road to the park.

Facilities: Picnic tables, toilets, hiking, nature trails, cross-country skiing.

Murwin Park

The shoreline of the Yahara River meanders along Murwin Park, providing a launch spot for canoeists who want to meet up with the connecting Rock River just downstream. The park's 40 acres include picnic tables, fireplaces and a wide diversity of birdlife.

Directions: Take Highway 184 to Fulton.

Facilities: Picnic tables, outhouses, canoe landing.

Royce-Dallman Park

This three-acre park serves primarily as an access to Lake Koshkonong for small fishing boats, but a picnic area is also provided.

Directions: From Milton, go north on Highway 26 to County N. Take County N east to North Charley Bluff Road and go north to the park.

Facilities: Picnic tables, toilets, boat landing.

Schollmeyer Park

Visitors can fish and launch their canoes on Turtle Creek at this half-acre site.

Directions: From Beloit, take County S (Shopiere Road) north just past its intersection with Hart Road.

Facilities: Canoe landing.

Sugar River Park

This heavily wooded, swampy park on the Sugar River provides a launch and take-out point for canoeists and boaters. Anglers will find an abundance of catfish and bullheads.

Directions: From Beloit, take Highway 81 west to South Nelson Road. Go south to the park.

Facilities: Picnic tables, boat landing.

Sweet-Allyn Park

Located on Turtle Creek southeast of Janesville, Sweet-Allyn Park offers a place to picnic, play softball and fish. The picnic area includes a shelter, tables, grills and electricity.

Directions: From Janesville, take Highway 51 south to Highway 351. Go east on Highway 351 to County J. Follow County J to the park at Shopiere.
Facilities: Picnic tables, picnic shelter, toilets, baseball, playground.

Walt Lindemann Sportsman's Park

This nine-acre park is popular for family picnics. It is home to the White-Tailed Deer Display and the County Cooperative Pheasant Rearing Project, both of which are open to viewing.

Directions: Take Highway 51 north from Janesville. The park is on the highway near its intersection with Highway 14.
Facilities: Picnic tables, picnic shelter, toilets, playground.

Summer wildflowers brighten park meadows and hiking paths.

RUSK COUNTY

Contact: Rusk County Forestry Department
311 East Miner Ave.
Ladysmith, WI 54848
(800) 535-RUSK, (715) 532-2113

Audie Flowage Park

Featuring a boat launch onto Audie Flowage, the park offers a picnic area including shelter, tables and a playground. Fifteen campsites with electrical hookups are available; when the campsites are full, visitors can go to the nearby Perch Lake Campground, the other part of the Audie Flowage-Perch Lake Recreational Area.

Directions: From Ladysmith, take Highway 8 west eight miles to Bruce. Turn north on County O and go 10 miles to Fire Lane Road. Turn north and travel four miles to Perch Lake Road. Turn west and proceed 1½ miles to the park.

Facilities: Picnic tables, picnic shelter, outhouses, tent sites, trailer sites, swimming, hiking, playground, boat landing.

Josie Creek Park

Bordered by Josie Creek and the Dairyland Reservoir, this park offers anglers the chance to hook muskellunge, walleye, large and smallmouth bass, catfish and pan fish from a boat landing and dock. A beach is also accessible, along with picnic and playground facilities. The park features 50-, 100- and 600-yard shooting ranges with benches and shelters. A 32-target, one-mile archery trail and 25 campsites are also available.

Directions: From Ladysmith, take Highway 8 east five miles to County X. Turn north and go three miles to the park.

Facilities: Picnic tables, picnic shelter, outhouses, tent sites, trailer sites, swimming, beach, hiking, playground.

Perch Lake Campground

A part of the Audie Flowage-Perch Lake Recreational Area, this campground has 16 campsites, along with a boat launch and access to the 1.5-mile Blue Hills Nature Trail. Cross-country ski trails are also accessible.

Directions: From Ladysmith, take Highway 8 west eight miles to Bruce. Turn north on County O and go 10 miles to Fire Lane Road. Turn north and travel four miles to Perch Lake Road. Turn west and proceed one mile to the campground.

Facilities: Picnic tables, outhouses, tent sites, swimming, cross-country skiing, boat landing.

ST. CROIX COUNTY

Contact: St. Croix County Parks Department
1049 Rustic Road 3
Glenwood City, WI 54013
(715) 265-4613

Apple River Property

A largely undeveloped 59-acre site, the property offers fishing and canoeing access to the Apple River.

Directions: From the junction of Highway 35 and Highway 64 in Somerset, take Highway 64 east to County C. Turn northeast on C and travel to the property access, which is just east of Huntington.

Facilities: Canoe access (no formal landing).

Glen Hills Park

The largest park in St. Croix County, Glen Hills County Park centers around Glen Lake, which is fed by Beaver Creek. The lake has a swimming beach. Anglers can fish for bluegills, trout and largemouth bass. Canoes, rowboats and paddleboats may be rented. Visitors also can hike a trail around the lake and picnic near the lake. Baseball, volleyball and horseshoe facilities, a playground and, during the winter, a cross-country ski trail are available. The park also features a 9-hole golf course with club and cart rental. The Glen Hills Golf Clubhouse offers food and cocktails and is open to the public. Sixty-one campsites are provided for overnight stays.

Directions: From Menomonie in Dunn County, take I-94 west 16 miles to the Glenwood City exit (Highway 128). Take Highway 128 north four miles to County E. Turn east and travel one mile to Rustic Road 3. Turn north and travel one mile to the campground entrance or two miles to the day-use entrance.

Facilities: Picnic tables, picnic shelter, outhouses, tent sites, trailer sites, swimming, beach, dressing rooms, hiking, cross-country skiing, baseball, volleyball, golf, playground, boat landing.

Pine Lake Park

Located on Pine Lake-Baldwin, this park offers a pleasant picnic spot, with a shelter and tables for visitor use. Mainly an angler's park, the site is open to pan fishing.

Directions: From the junction of I-94 and Highway 63, take Highway 63 north through Baldwin. Continue four miles past Baldwin to 110th Avenue. Turn west and go ½ mile to 205th Street. Turn north and go one mile to the park entrance.

Facilities: Picnic tables, picnic shelter, outhouses, boat landing.

Troy Park

Opening onto Lake St. Croix, of the scenic St. Croix River, this park contains a nice swimming beach and picnic tables.

Directions: From I-94 at Hudson, take the Carmichael Road exit. Go south and the road will turn into County F. Continue three miles and turn west on County FFF.

Facilities: Picnic tables, swimming, beach.

SAUK COUNTY

Contact: Sauk County Parks and Recreation
S7995 White Mound Drive
Hillpoint, WI 53937
(608) 546-5011

Hemlock Park

Used primarily for fishing on Hemlock Slough, the park provides picnic tables, a playground and a boat landing. It is also adjacent to the 400 Trail, a designated bike trail.

Directions: From Reedsburg, take Highway 33 northwest one mile onto Hemlock Drive. Go north on Hemlock Drive to Dutch Hollow Road. Turn west and go ⅛ mile to the park.

Facilities: Picnic tables, outhouses, playground, boat landing.

Lake Redstone Beach

This park features a swimming beach on Lake Redstone. It also has a picnic area with a shelter, tables and a playground. A fishing stream runs through the park.

Directions: From Reedsburg, take Highway 33 northeast to County V. Turn north and travel three miles to Douglas Road. Turn west and go one mile.

Facilities: Picnic tables, picnic shelter, outhouses, swimming, beach, dressing rooms, playground.

Lake Redstone Boat Landing

Providing boat access to Lake Redstone, the park offers a boat landing and pier.

Directions: From Reedsburg, take Highway 33 northeast to LaValle. In LaValle, turn north on Highway 58. Go about seven miles to County F. Turn east and travel four miles to LaValle Road. Turn south and continue to the landing.

Facilities: Toilets, boat landing.

Man Mound Park

The park features an Indian effigy mound, one of the only "man" mounds in Wisconsin. Picnic tables and a playground are available for visitor use.

Directions: From Baraboo, take Highway 33 east to County T. Turn north and go two miles to Man Mound Road. Turn east and continue four miles to the park.
Facilities: Picnic tables, outhouses, playground.

Sauk County Forest

The 600-acre Sauk County Forest offers hikers numerous unmarked firepaths for exploration.
Directions: From Lone Rock, take Highway 14 east one mile.
Facilities: Hiking.

Summer Oaks Boat Landing

The landing provides access to Lake Wisconsin, where anglers may hook fish native to the Wisconsin River.
Directions: From Sauk City, travel north 10 miles on Highway 78.
Facilities: Outhouses, boat landing.

White Mound Park

Located on White Mound Lake, the park offers a beach and boat landing for water enthusiasts. There is a one-mile nature trail and several horse trails through the park. Picnic areas with shelters and tables, a playground and a baseball diamond are provided. The park features 70 campsites, half of which have electricity. Special campsites for horseback riders are also available.
Directions: From Reedsburg, take Highway 23 south to County GG. Turn west and travel two miles to White Mound Drive. Turn north and continue to the park.
Facilities: Picnic tables, picnic shelter, outhouses, tent sites, trailer sites, swimming, beach, dressing rooms, hiking, nature trails, baseball, playground, boat landing.

Yellow Thunder Park

A ¼-acre park, this small prairie is dedicated to Chief Yellow Thunder.
Directions: From Baraboo, take County A north about four miles, ⅛ mile past the junction with Shady Lane Road.
Facilities: None.

SAWYER COUNTY

There are no county parks in Sawyer County.

SHAWANO COUNTY

Contact: Shawano County Park and Recreation Office
Courthouse, 311 N. Main St.
Shawano, WI 54166
(715) 526-5165

Hayman Falls Park

Located on Pella Pond, a part of the Embarrass River, this park offers 30 acres of wooded hiking trails, including a walk along the shoreline. The park also provides picnic tables, shelter and a playground.

Directions: From Shawano, travel west on Highway 29 to County U. Turn south and go two miles to County M. Turn west and travel 2½ miles to County D. Turn west on County D and travel two miles through Pella to Hayman Falls Road.

Facilities: Picnic tables, picnic shelter, outhouses, hiking, nature trails, playground.

Mielke Park

Featuring "the theatre in the woods," this park offers visitors four nature trails for quiet walks. Children can cast a line for pan fish in Mielke Pond. The site also provides picnic tables and a playground.

Directions: From the Shawano area, turn off Highway 29 onto County HHH, on the west side of Shawano. Turn north and continue 1½ miles.

Facilities: Picnic tables, outhouses, nature trails, playground.

Shawano County Park

A popular camping site with 90 campsites and an open field for trailer camping, Shawano County Park opens onto Shawano Lake. The lake provides a swimming beach, a boat landing and good bass fishing for daytime recreation. Visitors can also enjoy a roller rink in the community building, tennis courts and a playground.

Directions: From Highway 29 in Shawano, turn onto County H. Continue north six miles to Highway 29.

Facilities: Picnic tables, picnic shelter, toilets, tent sites, trailer sites, swimming, beach, dressing rooms, tennis, playground, boat landing.

Sunset Island Park

Situated in the city of Shawano, this island park offers picnic tables, picnic shelter and a boat landing.

Directions: Located two blocks off Highway 47/55 behind the Sheriff's Department, the park is on the channel between the Wolf River and Shawano Lake.
Facilities: Picnic tables, picnic shelter, boat landing.

Voelz Lake Memorial Park

This park is popular for its swimming beach on Wilson Lake. Located on the western edge of the county, the park also provides picnic tables and shelter, cross-country ski trails, a playground and a boat landing.
    Directions: From the junction of Highway 45 and Highway 29 in Wittenberg, take Highway 29 west four miles to Nightingale Road. Turn south and go one mile to Oak Road. Turn west and go ½ mile to the entrance.
    Facilities: Picnic tables, picnic shelter, outhouses, swimming, beach, cross-country skiing, playground, boat landing.

Waukechon Riverside Park

Offering access to the Wolf River, this park contains a boat landing and fishing piers. Although trout are most common, anglers can hook many different kinds of fish in the river.
    Directions: From Shawano, take Highway 22 south to County CC. Travel six miles south on CC to County CCC. Turn east and go ½ mile to the park.
    Facilities: Boat landing only.

SHEBOYGAN COUNTY

Contact: Sheboygan County Planning & Resources
                Department, Courthouse
                615 North Sixth St.
                Sheboygan, WI 53081
                (414) 459-3060

Broughton Sheboygan Marsh Park

Within the boundaries of this park lie the Sheboygan Marsh, Sheboygan River and Sheboygan Lake. These natural resources provide a beautiful backdrop for a day trip by canoe. Many visitors also take advantage of the park's beauty with an afternoon picnic or an evening around the campfire. The site includes 64 campsites, showers and a community lodge and restaurant. Winter visitors can enjoy a number of cross-country ski trails, while summer visitors will appreciate the playground and volleyball courts.

Directions: From Plymouth, take Highway 67 north to Elkhart Lake. In Elkhart Lake, take County A west to County J. Continue one mile northwest on County J to the park.

Facilities: Picnic tables, picnic shelter, toilets, tent sites, trailer sites, cross-country skiing, volleyball, playground, boat landing.

Crystal Lake Access

This 114-acre lake is heavily used for fishing and boating. An extensively developed shoreline and fishing pier allow anglers to cast their lines for northern, crappie, perch, walleye, bass and bluegills. Many visitors enjoy boating on this lake, but no motorboats are allowed on Sundays.

Directions: From the junction of Highway 23 and County C just west of Plymouth, travel north 3½ miles on County C.

Facilities: Outhouses, boat landing.

Elkhart Lake Access

At 300 acres and a maximum depth of 110 feet, Elkhart Lake is the largest natural lake in the county and the fourth deepest in the state. Its clear waters make it an excellent spot for boating and swimming, and anglers are likely to hook smallmouth bass, rock bass and, with some luck, walleye from the fishing pier. No motorboats are allowed on Sundays.

Directions: From Plymouth, take Highway 23 west to County P. Turn north and travel five miles to the access.

Facilities: Outhouses, boat landing.

Gerber Lakes Access

A largely undeveloped 22-acre system of two basins connected by a navigable channel, Gerber Lakes provides a wilderness site for nonmotorized boaters and anglers looking for bass, bluegills, crappie and perch. A fishing pier provides shoreline access to the waters.

Directions: From the junction of Highway 23 and Highway 57 just east of Plymouth, travel north on Highway 57 for 3½ miles to Gerber Lake Road. Turn west and go ¾ mile.

Facilities: Outhouses, boat landing.

Jetzer's Lake Access

This 15-acre lake is known for its family fishing opportunities. From the fishing pier, young anglers can hook small bluegills and black crappies, while more experienced anglers may catch bass and northern pike. Nonmotorized boats are also allowed on the lake, and picnic tables are provided.

Directions: From Sheboygan, take Highway 42 northwest into Howards Grove. Turn west on County A and travel two miles to the landing.
Facilities: Picnic tables, outhouses, boat landing.

Little Elkhart Lake Access
A scenic 48-acre lake, Little Elkhart offers great fishing for bass, bluegill, northern pike and walleye. Visitors can also enjoy a picnic or boating on the lake, although motorboats are not allowed on Sundays.
Directions: From the junction of Highway 23 and Highway 67 at Plymouth, travel three miles north on Highway 67 to Schwaller Drive. Turn northeast across from the entrance to Road America and continue to the park.
Facilities: Picnic tables, outhouses, boat landing.

Taylor Park
Located in the city of Sheboygan, this park provides a wooded picnic area with picnic tables and a playground. A picnic shelter with toilets is on the grounds, but can only be used by reservation.
Directions: Take Highway 23 into Sheboygan to Taylor Drive. Turn south and continue to the junction with Erie Avenue.
Facilities: Picnic tables, picnic shelter, toilets, playground.

TAYLOR COUNTY

Contact: Taylor County Recreation Director
Courthouse
224 South 2nd St.
Medford, WI 54451
(715) 748-1486

Chelsea Lake Recreation Area
Known for its excellent fishing and boating, Chelsea Lake provides a boat landing and a handicapped-accessible fishing pier, as well as a picturesque picnic spot.
Directions: From Medford, take Highway 13 north eight miles to Chelsea Avenue. Turn west and go ¼ mile on Chelsea Avenue to Fisher Creek Road. Turn north and go one mile to Chelsea Lake Lane, then proceed west ¼ mile.
Facilities: Picnic tables, picnic shelter, outhouses, boat landing.

Diamond Lake Public Recreation Area

Diamond Lake contains a beach, boat landing and fishing pier. Visitors looking for a picnic site can use the picnic tables or handicapped-accessible shelter, while children can amuse themselves on the playground.

Directions: From Lublin, travel north about three miles on County F. Then turn east on Diamond Drive and continue one mile to the park.

Facilities: Picnic tables, picnic shelter, toilets, swimming, beach, playground, boat landing.

Lion's Memorial Park

The Chequamegon Waters Flowage, known for its excellent fishing, is directly adjacent to Lion's Memorial Park. Anglers can hook bass, northern pike, crappie and bluegill in the flowage waters. Situated on a small peninsula in the Chequamegon National Forest, the park is also a nice picnic spot, offering tables and a shelter.

Directions: From Gilman, take Highway 73 north five miles to County M. Turn east and travel three miles to County G. Then go ½ mile south.

Facilities: Picnic tables, picnic shelter, outhouses, boat landing.

Miller Dam Park and Boat Landing

Located in the Chequamegon National Forest, Miller Dam Park offers a concrete boat landing and boating pier to access the Chequamegon Waters Flowage. The flowage also gives anglers an excellent chance to catch bass, northern pike, crappie and bluegill. The park includes picnic tables, an open shelter and handicapped-accessible toilets.

Directions: From Gilman, take Highway 73 north two miles to County G. Turn east and continue four miles to the park.

Facilities: Picnic tables, picnic shelter, toilets, boat landing.

Sackett Lake Public Recreation Area

Known primarily for its excellent swimming beach and picnic areas, Sackett Lake has a shelter with concessions and a bathhouse with dressing rooms. The park also contains a boat landing and a playground and provides good fishing.

Directions: From Medford, take Highway 64 west three miles to County E. Turn north and continue four miles to County M. Turn west and go ½ mile to Sackett Lake Drive. Then proceed north ½ mile.

Facilities: Picnic tables, picnic shelter, toilets, swimming, beach, dressing rooms, playground, boat landing.

Taylor County Forest

Separated into three sections in the northeast corner of Taylor County, the county forest provides access to the Ice Age Hiking Trail and a multitude of snowmobile/ATV trails. Visitors can also find excellent trout fishing on the Camp 8 Flowage, along with picnic tables and campsites for tents and trailers.

Directions: From Rib Lake, take Highway 102 east two miles to Wilderness Avenue. Proceed east three miles to the park.

Facilities: Picnic tables, outhouses, tent sites, trailer sites, hiking.

Wellington Lake Park

Although it is a small park, Wellington Lake offers a swimming beach, boat landing and fishing.

Directions: From Rib Lake, travel 2½ miles west on Highway 102 to Wellington Lake Drive. Then turn south and continue 1½ miles to the park.

Facilities: Outhouses, swimming, beach, boat landing.

Wood Lake Public Recreation Area

Located in the Taylor County Forest, this park is popular with visitors because of serene Wood Lake, which is a great spot for canoeing or paddle-boating. Its clear waters and excellent beach also provide a fine place to swim. No motors are allowed on the lake. Picnic areas and six campsites are available.

Directions: From Rib Lake, go three miles east on Highway 102. Turn east on Wood Lake Avenue and continue three miles to the park.

Facilities: Picnic tables, toilets, tent sites, trailer sites, swimming, beach, dressing rooms, hiking, playground, boat landing.

TREMPEALEAU COUNTY

Contact: Trempealeau County Tourism Council
County Courthouse
Box 67
Whitehall, WI 54773
(715) 538-2311

Farm Progress Days Park

Farm Progess Days Park is used primarily for picnics and as a day-use park. It has a fishing pond, tennis courts and a baseball diamond.

Directions: The park is located directly off Highway 121 three miles east of Independence or two miles west of Whitehall.

Facilities: Picnic tables, picnic shelter, outhouses, baseball, tennis.

Pietrek Park

This park is known for its camping facilities, used primarily for group camping. It also has a self-guided nature trail and picnic areas.

Directions: The park is located directly off Highway 93 five miles south of Independence and four miles north of Arcadia.

Facilities: Picnic tables, picnic shelter, outhouses, tent sites, nature trails.

VERNON COUNTY

Contact: Vernon County Clerk's Office
Courthouse Annex
Viroqua, WI 54665
(608) 637-3569

Blackhawk Recreation Area

Spend a little time here picnicking or fishing the Mississippi and you'll likely spot an eagle or two flying overhead. Partly owned by the county and partly by the Army Corps of Engineers, this rural park provides a peaceful spot for camping and opportunities to swim and boat the river. The boat dock is handicapped accessible.

Directions: From La Crosse, take Highway 35 south through Victory. Turn west on County BI.

Facilities: Picnic tables, picnic shelter, outhouses, tent sites, trailer sites, swimming, beach, playground.

Jersey Valley Park

Manmade Jersey Valley Lake is a popular fishing spot, and the park provides a handicapped-accessible fishing pier. The day-use park also includes a picnic area, a playground and a four-mile hiking trail that encircles the park.

Directions: From the junction of Highway 14/61 and Highway 27 in Westby, take Highway 27 north to County X. Turn east on County X and continue to the park.

Facilities: Picnic tables, picnic shelter, outhouses, swimming, hiking, playground, boat landing.

Rentz Memorial Park (Esofea Park)

Used minimally by campers, Rentz Memorial Park (also known as Esofea Park), draws local residents for picnicking and recreation. A playground and five small fishing ponds provide opportunities for children.

Directions: From La Crosse, take Highway 14-61 east to County B, just past Coon Valley. Turn south on B and continue to Esofea.

Facilities: Picnic tables, picnic shelter, outhouses, tent sites, trailer sites, baseball, playground.

Sidie Hollow Park

You can pitch a tent almost anywhere in this secluded park, choosing either open field or more rugged, primitive surroundings. A hiking trail encircles Sidie Hollow Lake, a small manmade lake used frequently by anglers and boaters.

Directions: From Viroqua, take Highway 56 west to County XX. Turn south and continue to the park.

Facilities: Picnic tables, picnic shelter, outhouses, tent sites, trailer sites, hiking, playground, boat landing.

VILAS COUNTY

Contact: Vilas County Forestry Department
Courthouse
P.O. Box 369,
Eagle River, WI 54521
(715) 479-5160

Baker Lake Landing

Located in Vilas County Forest, this park provides a fishing pier and boat landing onto small Baker Lake.

Directions: From Conover, take County K west about two miles to County S. Turn north and travel about one mile to Baker Lake Road. Turn west and travel approximately two miles to the lake.

Facilities: Boat landing only.

Black Oak Lake Landing

This landing, adjacent to Black Oak Lake Park, offers a spot off the water for boaters to rest. The site has a portable pier and grills.

Directions: From Conover, take County K west about two miles to County S. Turn north on S and continue until it comes to a T intersection at County B. Turn east on County B and continue to the landing.
Facilities: Boat landing only.

Black Oak Lake Park

Located on the northern border of lake-speckled Vilas County, this park features a sand beach on the shore of Black Oak Lake. The lake's deep, clear waters also offer anglers a chance to catch pike, walleye and large and smallmouth bass. Visitors can enjoy a picnic on the water's edge or toss horseshoes into the pits provided.
Directions: From Conover, take County K west about two miles to County S. Turn north on S and continue until it comes to a T intersection at County B. Turn east on County B and continue to the landing.
Facilities: Picnic tables, outhouses, swimming, beach.

Boot Lake Landing

This county forest site offers a fishing pier and boat launch onto Boot Lake.
Directions: From Eagle River, take Highway 32/45 north to County G. Turn west and travel about 2½ miles to Boot Lake Road. Turn north and continue to the lake.
Facilities: Boat landing only.

Buckatabon Campsite

Canoeists traveling down the Wisconsin River often camp at this site after a day's travel. The site offers two canoe-accessible campsites with a picnic table, grills and a shelter.
Directions: Canoeists will find the site at the point where the Buckatabon River and the Wisconsin River meet. Bicyclists can reach the site by taking County K west of Conover to E. Buckatabon Road, turning south and then turning east on the county forest road after the Buckatabon River.
Facilities: Picnic table, picnic shelter, outhouses, tent sites.

Buckatabon Lake Landing

Located on the south shore of Upper Buckatabon Lake, the site has a boat landing and a fishing pier, along with a picnic table, grill and fire ring.
Directions: From Conover, take County K west about two miles to E. Buckatabon Road. Turn south and follow Buckatabon to the lake.
Facilities: Picnic table, boat landing.

Conover Shooting Range

This shooting range offers seven backstops and eight firing points on a five-acre parcel of county forest land.

Directions: From Eagle River, take Highway 32/45 north past Lake of the Hills to Range Road. Turn northeast to the range.

Facilities: None.

Decker Lake Hunter Hiking Trail

This county forest unit offers a 3.1-mile game trail, which is used by hunters, hikers, mountain bikers and cross-country skiers.

Directions: From Conover, take County K west.

Facilities: Hiking, cross-country skiing.

Deep Lake Pier and Hunter Hiking Trail

Featuring a handicapped-accessible floating pier system, this site offers a pan-fishing pier and granite ramp. The unit also has 4.95 miles of game trail, which is used for hunting, hiking, mountain biking and cross-country skiing. A picnic table, grill and fire ring are also provided.

Directions: From Eagle River, take Highway 32/45 north to County G. Turn west and travel about 2½ miles to Boot Lake Road. Just before Boot Lake, turn north on Hunter Lake Road. Follow Hunter Lake about two miles to Deep Lake Road. Turn south and continue to the lake.

Facilities: Picnic table, hiking, cross-country skiing.

Dr. Oldfield Park

A memorial to former resident Dr. Oldfield, this park contains a boat landing, picnic tables and grills on two acres of county forest land.

Directions: From Eagle River, travel ½ mile north on Highway 45 to County G. Turn west and travel ¼ mile to the park.

Facilities: Picnic tables, outhouses, boat landing.

Eagle Lake Park

This park is situated on the Eagle River chain of lakes, the world's largest chain of inland lakes. Eagle Lake, one of the 27 connected lakes, provides a great spot for boats, canoes and pontoons. A swimming beach is also available on 440 feet of lakefront area, and anglers can hook muskellunge, walleye and smallmouth bass. Visitors can also test the water from a recreational pier or enjoy a picnic using the tables, grills and shelter provided.

Directions: From Eagle River, travel 1½ miles north on Highway 45 to Chain O'Lakes Road. Turn east and travel one mile to the park, which is on the right.

Facilities: Picnic tables, picnic shelter, outhouses, swimming, beach.

Eagle Lake Landing

Adjacent to Eagle Lake Park, this site has a boat landing and portable pier.
Directions: From Eagle River, travel 1½ miles north on Highway 45 to Chain O'Lakes Road. Turn east and travel one mile to the landing on the right.
Facilities: Boat landing only.

Heart Lake Hunter Hiking Trail

The site offers a multipurpose game trail in the woods just south of Heart Lake. There is also a canoe landing on the Wisconsin River at this site.
Directions: From Conover, take Highway 32/45 north to Rummels Road. Turn west and go to Heart Lake Road. Turn south and continue to the trail.
Facilities: Tent site, hiking, cross-country skiing, canoe landing.

Hunter Lake Beach and Picnic Area

Hunter Lake provides a scenic backdrop for a swim or a picnic, facilitated by tables, grills and fire rings. The site also includes horseshoe pits, a swimming beach, a playground and a boat landing.
Directions: From Eagle River, take Highway 32/45 north to County G. Turn west and travel about 2½ miles to Boot Lake Road. Just before Boot Lake, turn north on Hunter Lake Road. Follow this north to the lake.
Facilities: Picnic tables, outhouses, swimming, beach, playground, boat landing.

Lac Vieux Desert Park

While anglers can look for muskellunge, pike and walleye in the waters of Lac Vieux Desert, the main attraction here is the headwaters of the Wisconsin River. So small visitors can almost jump across it, the beginning of the river makes an excellent place for the more adventurous to embark on a canoe trip in waters suitable for beginners. The site also provides picnic tables and grills.
Directions: From Conover, take Highway 32/45 north to County E. Turn east and go to FR 2205. Turn north and continue to the park.
Facilities: Picnic tables, outhouses.

Lake of the Hills Landing

This county forest unit offers a pan-fishing pier and boat landing onto Lake of the Hills. The lake is the source for Sucker Creek, which flows into the Wisconsin River.
Directions: From Eagle River, take Highway 32/45 north to the county forest boundary. Turn east on Lake Hills Landing Road.
Facilities: Boat landing only.

Lake of the Woods Campsite

This walk-in campsite offers hikers a single-unit site with a picnic table and fire ring.

Directions: From Conover, take County K west two miles to County S. Turn north on County S and travel about one mile to Baker Lake Road. Continue on Baker Lake to the western boundary of the county forest. Turn northeast on White Squaw Lake Road and continue north about three miles to the lake.
Facilities: Picnic table, tent site.

Langley Lake Hunter Hiking Trail

This county forest site features 15.7 miles of multipurpose game trail for the hiker, biker and hunter. One and a half miles of game trail are handicapped accesssible. The unit also has 5.3 miles of groomed ski trails in the winter.

Directions: From Conover, take County K west to the lake on the far west side of the forest.
Facilities: Hiking, cross-country skiing.

Mud Minnow Lake Hunter Hiking Trail

The 2.8 miles of multipurpose game trail on county forest land wind close to small Mud Minnow Lake.

Directions: From Eagle River, take Highway 32/45 north to County G. Turn west and continue to the trail area.
Facilities: Hiking, cross-country skiing.

Muskellunge Lake Landing

Located on the northern tip of Muskellunge Lake, the site features a catwalk for boat launching and a boat landing.

Directions: From Eagle River, take Highway 32/45 north to County G. Turn west and continue to Balsam Lane. Turn south.
Facilities: Boat landing only.

Muskrat Creek Hunter Hiking Trail and Landing

This site offers six miles of multipurpose game trail along Muskrat Creek. A canoe landing is also provided on Muskrat Creek.

Directions: From Conover, take County K east about 2½ miles to Muskrat Road. Turn north and continue.
Facilities: Hiking, cross-country skiing, canoe landing.

Pioneer Creek Hunter Hiking Trail

The 7.35 miles of multipurpose game trail at this park form a loop to a canoe landing on Pioneer Creek.

Directions: From Conover in the heart of Vilas County Forest, take County K east to the trail area.
Facilities: Hiking, cross-country skiing, canoe landing.

Razorback Road Campsite

For those touring the Wisconsin River by canoe, this single campsite offers a primitive wayside along the river, with a tent site and picnic table.
Directions: Canoeists will find the site on the Wisconsin River, just south of the fork with Portage Creek. The site is also accessible to bicyclists: Take Highway 32/45 north of Conover to Rummels Road, turn west and then turn north on Razorback Road.
Facilities: Picnic table, tent site.

River Road Campsite

This canoe-in camping area has two campsites with picnic tables, three grills and three fire rings.
Directions: Canoeists will find this site on the Wisconsin River, south of the fork with Buckatabon River. Bicyclists can access the site by taking Highway 32/45 south of Conover to River Road and turning west.
Facilities: Outhouses, tent sites.

Riverside Park

This small park is generally used for overflow from the fairgrounds, but it also offers a shoreline view of the Eagle River.
Directions: From Eagle River, travel toward the river ¼ mile on River Road.
Facilities: Toilets.

Rummels Road Campsite

This canoe-in camping area on the Wisconsin River has two campsites, grills, a picnic table, shelter and fire ring.
Directions: Canoeists will find the site on the Wisconsin River, just after it passes under Rummels Road. Bicyclists can access the site by taking Highway 32/45 north of Conover and turning east on Rummels Road.
Facilities: Picnic table, picnic shelter, outhouses, tent sites.

Ski Hill Hunter Hiking Trail

This county forest unit provides 5.1 miles of multipurpose game trail.
Directions: From Eagle River, take Highway 32/45 north, just past the county forest boundary. Turn east on Ski Hill Road.
Facilities: Hiking, cross-country skiing.

Snipe Lake and Ewald Lake Hunter Hiking Trail

The largest unit in the county forest game trail system, this site offers 16.4 miles of multipurpose game trail. The unit also provides a portable pier, shelter, picnic tables and grills.

> **Directions:** From Eagle River, take Highway 70 west along the Wisconsin River to Wilderness Trail Road, just after Sunset Lake Road. Travel north.
> **Facilities:** Picnic tables, outhouses, hiking, cross-country skiing.

Tamarack Springs Boat Landing

This site provides boating access onto Tamarack Flowage, a scenic water area that is the source for Tamarack Creek, which flows into the Wisconsin River. A fishing pier is available.

> **Directions:** From Conover, take County K west about two miles to County S. Turn north and continue to the landing.
> **Facilities:** Boat landing only.

Tamarack Springs Park

Popular with campers and trout fishers, this park provides access to Tamarack Creek. Seven campsites are offered, each with a picnic table and fire ring.

> **Directions:** From Conover, take County K west about two miles to County S. Turn north and continue to Tamarack Road. Turn north and follow to the park, located on the north side of the creek.
> **Facilities:** Picnic tables, outhouses, tent sites.

Tamarack Springs Picnic Area and Landing

This semiremote park, across the creek from Tamarack Springs Park, has a canoe landing, picnic tables and grills.

> **Directions:** From Conover, take County K west about two miles to County S. Turn north and continue to Tamarack Road. Turn north and follow Tamarack Road to the picnic area, located on the south side of the creek.
> **Facilities:** Picnic tables, outhouses, canoe landing.

Torch Lake Beach and Picnic Area

Along with 6.5 miles of multipurpose game trail, this site also offers a swimming beach on Torch Lake, along with picnic tables, grills, horseshoe pits and a playground.

> **Directions:** From Conover, travel south on Highway 32/45 to Torch Lake Road. Turn west and continue to the park.
> **Facilities:** Picnic tables, outhouses, swimming, beach, hiking, cross-country skiing, playground.

White Spruce Campsite and Hunter Hiking Trail

This walk-in camping area has a single site with picnic table and fire ring. A multipurpose game trail is also provided.

Directions: From Conover, take County K west two miles to County S. Turn north on County S and travel about one mile to Baker Lake Road. Continue on Baker Lake to the western boundary of the county forest. Turn northeast on White Squaw Lake Road and continue north about two miles to the game trail and lake.

Facilities: Picnic table, tent site, hiking, cross-country skiing.

White Squaw Lake Hunter Hiking Trail

This county forest unit provides 8.7 miles of multipurpose game trails for hikers, mountain bikers, hunters and cross-country skiers.

Directions: From Conover in the heart of Vilas County Forest, take County K west two miles to County S. Turn north on County S and travel about one mile to Baker Lake Road. Continue on Baker Lake to the western boundary of the county forest. Turn northeast on White Squaw Lake Road.

Facilities: Hiking, cross-country skiing.

Wood Duck Lake Hunter Hiking Trail

This site offers access to Wood Duck Lake from a walk-in fishing pier, as well as access to multipurpose game trails.

Directions: From Eagle River, take Highway 70 west along the Wisconsin River to Wilderness Trail Road, just past Sunset Lake Road. Turn north.

Facilities: Hiking, cross-country skiing.

WALWORTH COUNTY

Contact: Walworth County Highway Department
W4097 County Road NN
Elkhorn, WI 53121
(414) 741-3114

Natureland Park

Natureland County Park features natural kettles, artesian wells, a bog area, lowland vegetation, wooded areas and plenty of wildlife. The park offers a picturesque spot for picnics and hiking on the nature trail.

Directions: From Whitewater, take Highway 89 south about six miles to Territorial Road. Turn west and continue to the park.

Facilities: Picnic tables, picnic shelter, outhouses, hiking, nature trails.

WASHBURN COUNTY

Contact: Washburn County Forest
850 W. Beaver Brook Ave., Suite #4
Spooner, WI 54801
(715) 635-2886

Leisure Lake Picnic Area

This small picnic area, located near part of the St. Croix National Scenic Riverway, offers a swimming beach, boat landing and picnic areas on Leisure Lake.

Directions: From Spooner, take County K north about five miles to Spring Lake Road. Turn west and continue to the stop sign, where Spring Lake Road turns into Island Lake Road. Turn north and travel about three miles to Skunk Lake Road, which will be marked with signs for Washburn County Youth Camp. Turn to the right and continue to the park.

Facilities: Picnic tables, outhouses, swimming, beach, boat landing.

Sawmill Lake Campground

Located on 5,000 acres of county forest land, this primitive campground offers 20 campsites on the east shore of Sawmill Lake. The site also provides swimming, a small open-air pavilion, a boat landing and a nature trail winding through the woods. Twenty-eight lakes are scattered within a one-mile radius of the campground.

Directions: From Spooner, take Highway 70 east 15 miles to County B. Turn south on County B and go three miles, then continue south on Birchwood Fire Lane for five miles.

Facilities: Picnic tables, outhouses, tent sites, trailer sites, swimming, hiking, nature trail, boat landing.

Slim Creek Flowage and Picnic Area

This site on the Slim Creek flowage provides opportunities for boating and fishing. Anglers can hook northern, walleye, pan fish and bass. Visitors can also picnic near the water.

Directions: From Spooner, take Highway 70 east 15 miles to County B. Turn south on County B and go 2¾ miles to Slim Creek. Turn down Slim Creek and go one mile to the picnic area.

Facilities: Picnic tables, boat landing.

Totogatic Park

The Minong Flowage makes for a scenic camping area at this park. About ¾ of the 75 campsites are located on the shoreline, so campers can tie their boats right up to their campsites. Half of the sites provide electricity. The park has a boat launch and a swimming beach. A fish-cleaning house allows anglers to clean up their catch, which could include northern, walleye, pan fish and bass. A nature trail also winds through the park, and picnic tables, an open-air pavilion and a playground are available.

Directions: From Spooner, travel north 22 miles on Highway 53 to Minong. In Minong, turn west on Highway 77 and travel one mile to County I. Turn north and go seven miles to the park entrance.

Facilities: Picnic tables, outhouses, toilets, tent sites, trailer sites, swimming, beach, hiking, nature trail, playground, boat landing.

Re-enactors hold the Bloody Lake Rendezvous the first weekend in May at Blackhawk Memorial Park in Lafayette County.

WASHINGTON COUNTY

Contact: Washington County Land Use
and Park Department
333 E. Washington St.
West Bend, WI 53095
(414) 335-4445

Cedar Lake Wayside

This three-acre park provides picnic tables and grills in a small rest area.

Directions: From West Bend, take Highway 33 west two miles to County Z. Turn south and go 3½ miles to County NN. Turn east and continue to the entrance.
Facilities: Picnic tables, outhouses.

Glacier Hills Park

This picturesque site, close to Freiss Lake, provides good views of Holy Hill, especially in autumn. The chapel on the site, once part of a church camp, is now the setting for many weddings. Visitors take advantage of the view by hiking or picnicking. A nature center is run by the Kettle Moraine Audubon Society.
Directions: From West Bend, take Highway 45 south 10 miles to Highway 167. Turn west and drive 5½ miles to Freiss Lake Road. Turn south and continue to the park entrance.
Facilities: Picnic tables, picnic shelter, outhouses, toilets, hiking, cross-country skiing, baseball, volleyball, playground.

Groeden Park

Situated in the flood plain of the Milwaukee River, this park provides a spot for fishing and picnicking. A shelter, tables and grills are available, along with a playground. Canoeists can access the Milwaukee River from a pier in the park. All facilities are handicapped accessible.
Directions: From West Bend, head east on Highway 33 for 4½ miles to County M. Turn south to the park entrance.
Facilities: Picnic tables, picnic shelter, outhouses, playground, boat landing.

Heritage Trails

An old farm site, this park now contains hiking trails that wind through the park and around a small pond. Picnic tables, a shelter and a playground, all handicapped accessible, are available.
Directions: From Hartford, take Highway 60 east to Highway 175. Turn southeast and continue one mile to County J. Turn south and go one mile to County E. Turn west and go ¾ mile to the park entrance.
Facilities: Picnic tables, picnic shelter, outhouses, hiking, playground.

Homestead Hollow Park

A barn on this former farm site now serves as a picnic shelter. Picnic tables, a playground and a baseball diamond are also provided.
Directions: From West Bend, travel south 10 miles on Highway 45 to Highway 167. Turn west and go one mile to County Y. Turn south and go one mile to Friestadt Road. Turn east and continue to the park.
Facilities: Picnic tables, picnic shelter, outhouses, baseball, playground.

Lizard Mound Park

This park is known for its Indian effigy mounds, accessible by hiking a short trail. There are also picnic tables.

Directions: From West Bend, take Highway 144 north two miles to County A. Turn east and travel one mile to the park entrance.

Facilities: Picnic tables, outhouses, hiking, nature trails.

Ridge Run Park

A small creek runs through this park, and three lakes are located within its parameters. Two of the lakes, Wells Lake and Boot Lake, are in a stocking program for rainbow trout. A third small lake, Pick Lake, enhances the view for those enjoying the picnic areas or playground facilities. Hiking, cross-country skiing, tobogganing and sledding on a lighted hill are winter activities.

Directions: Located in West Bend city limits, the park can be reached by taking Highway 33 west to University Drive and then traveling south a couple of blocks.

Facilities: Picnic tables, picnic shelter, outhouses, hiking, cross-country skiing, playground.

Sandy Knoll Park

Spring wildflowers cover the rolling terrain of this park, which features an old barn converted into a picnic shelter. A manmade pond stocked with rainbow trout, bluegill and other fish offers fishing. The park also provides a baseball diamond, a soccer field, basketball courts, a playground and a swimming beach with dressing rooms.

Directions: From West Bend, take Highway 33 east one mile to Trenton Road. Turn north and travel two miles to Wallace Lake Road. Turn east and continue to the park.

Facilities: Picnic tables, picnic shelter, outhouses, swimming, beach, dressing rooms, cross-country skiing, baseball, playground.

WAUKESHA COUNTY

Contact: Waukesha County Park and Planning Department
Administration Center
1320 Pewaukee Road
Waukesha, WI 53188
(414) 548-7801

Ashippun Lake Access

This site provides fishing and boating access onto Ashippun Lake, along with picnic tables for the day visitor. A public-funded snowmobile trail runs through the site.

> **Directions:** From Oconomowoc, take Highway 67 north 3½ miles to McMahon Road. Turn east and travel 1½ miles to the access drive.
> **Facilities:** Picnic tables, outhouses, boat landing.

Eble Park Ice Arena

A facility specifically for ice skating, the arena offers concessions, lockers and meeting rooms.

> **Directions:** From the junction of I-94 and Highway 18 in Brookfield, take Highway 18 (Bluemound Road) east 1¼ miles.
> **Facilities:** Toilets.

Menomonee Park

The sparkling clear water of 16-acre Menomonee Quarry Lake provides great opportunities for scuba diving, swimming and fishing. Hikers, skiers, snowmobilers and horseback riders will find trails throughout the 397 acres of rolling fields, maple woods, cattail marshes and wetlands. An interpretive nature trail leads to Camp Pow Wow, an area for the mentally and physically handicapped residents of Waukesha County. Those looking for longer trail adventures can access the 12-mile Waukesha County Bugline Recreation Trail and a public-funded snowmobile trail. Other facilities include volleyball, archery, picnic areas and 31 campsites and group camping areas.

> **Directions:** From Menomonee Falls, take Highway 74 southwest past Lannon to County V (Town Line Road). Turn north and travel 1½ miles.
> **Facilities:** Picnic tables, picnic shelter, outhouses, toilets, tent sites, trailer sites, swimming, beach, dressing rooms, hiking, nature trails, cross-country skiing, volleyball.

Minooka Park

The name of this park is derived from a Native American word meaning "maple forest" or "good earth," appropriately describing the wooded hills and rich fields of the site. A four-acre swimming and fishing pond is a major summer attraction, along with opportunities for nature study, hiking and horseback riding through the woods. In the winter, visitors come for the sledding hill and cross-country ski trails, which are groomed weekly. Picnic areas are provided throughout the park, along with facilities for baseball, volleyball, soccer and archery. A group camp site is also available.

Directions: From Waukesha, take Racine Avenue (County Y) southeast to Sunset Drive. Turn west and continue to the park.
Facilities: Picnic tables, picnic shelter, outhouses, toilets, swimming, beach, dressing rooms, hiking, nature trails, cross-country skiing, baseball, volleyball.

Moor Downs Golf Course

Located in Waukesha, the golf course provides a clubhouse with concessions, lockers, a Pro Shop, meeting space and dining areas.
Directions: In Waukesha, take Delafield Street about ½ mile south of Moreland Boulevard to Prospect Avenue. Turn east on Prospect.
Facilities: Toilets, golf.

Mukwonago Park

This park features a 16-acre spring-fed lake that offers a pleasant setting for picnics. Formed during the last glacial period, a high ridge covered with pre-settlement vegetation provides a lofty view of the rolling terrain. Other facilities include a nature trail, a baseball diamond, swimming pond, snowmobile trail and sledding hill. More than 30 campsites are available.
Directions: From the junction of Highway 83 and Highway 99 in Mukwonago, take Highway 99 west 2½ miles.
Facilities: Picnic tables, picnic shelter, outhouses, tent sites, trailer sites, swimming, beach, dressing rooms, hiking, nature trails, baseball.

Muskego Park

In the summer, the major attraction at this park is the swimming beach on a one-acre manmade pond. Hikers, skiers and horseback riders will find trails winding through the park, connecting to trails in the Muskego Park Hardwoods State Scientific Area. Visitors will also find facilities for baseball, volleyball, tennis and horseshoes, along with picnic areas and 24 campsites.
Directions: From the junction of County Y and County L in Muskego, take County L west ¾ mile to the park.
Facilities: Picnic tables, picnic shelter, outhouses, toilets, tent sites, trailer sites, swimming, beach, dressing rooms, hiking, cross-country skiing, baseball, volleyball, tennis.

Naga-Waukee Park, Golf Course and Ice Arena

Water enthusiasts appreciate access to Lake Nagawicka, which is used for swimming, fishing, sailing, waterskiing, power boating and canoeing. Visitors can also access Pewaukee Lake from the east side of the 18-hole Lawrence Packard golf course, which includes a clubhouse with food service, locker rooms, a Pro Shop and indoor and outdoor dining. Hikers can take the foot path through the park, and the more adventurous can start a trek on the Ice Age Trail, which runs through the park. The park offers 33 campsites for overnight visitors, along with a boat landing and baseball and volleyball facilities. Adjacent to the park is the Naga-Waukee Ice Arena, which has concessions, lockers and meeting rooms.

Directions: East of Delafield, exit I-94 at Highway 83. To reach the park, continue ½ mile north on Highway 83. To reach the golf course, continue north on Highway 83 from I-94 to the stoplights on Golf Road. Turn east on Golf Road and go to County E. Turn north on County E and travel ½ mile to the entrance. To reach the ice arena, continue north on Highway 83 from I-94 to the stoplights on Golf Road. Turn west on Golf Road.

Facilities: Picnic tables, picnic shelter, outhouses, toilets, tent sites, trailer sites, swimming, beach, hiking, baseball, volleyball, golf, boat landing.

Nashotah Park

At 443 acres, this park is the largest in the county. It contains six short but scenic hiking trails that wind through eight landscape types created by the last glacier: a natural lake system, an oak forest, an oak savannah, a cedar glade, a floating leaf marsh, a meadow, a shallow marsh and a deep marsh. Grass Lake and Forest Lake create a setting perfect for picnics; a shelter, tables and grills are available. Two baseball diamonds, horseshoe pits and a sledding hill are also on the site.

Directions: From Oconomowoc, take Highway 16 east to County C. Turn south and continue to the park, which is ½ mile north of Nashotah.

Facilities: Picnic tables, picnic shelter, toilets, hiking, nature trails, cross-country skiing, baseball, volleyball.

Nemahbin Lake Access

This eight-acre landing provides fishing, boating and waterskiing access to Nemahbin Lake.

Directions: Exit I-94 at Sawyer Road (County P), just east of Oconomowoc. Go south and turn east on County DR. Go ¼ mile to the landing.

Facilities: Outhouses, boat landing.

Pewaukee Lake Access

This site provides access to the west end of Pewaukee Lake, and has drinking water, soda machines and picnic tables.

Directions: From I-94 east of Delafield, exit onto County E. Turn north and travel one mile to the landing.

Facilities: Toilets, boat landing.

Retzer Nature Center

This 335-acre site originated with a 90-acre piece of land tended by John and Florence Retzer, who reportedly hand-planted more than 26,000 trees, shrubs and flowers to restore the land after its many years as a farm. Since then, many acres have been added and a nature center building has been built. The center has nature displays, merchandise sales, meeting rooms, a lab, greenhouse and work room. Visitors can enjoy the outdoor education area by hiking five trails, including an 800-foot-long handicapped-accessible paved trail. A cross-country ski trail is also available in the winter, and outdoor tables are provided for group use.

Directions: From Waukesha, take Highway 18 west 3½ miles to County DT. Turn south on County DT to the center's entrance.

Facilities: Toilets, hiking, nature trails, cross-country skiing.

School Section Lake Access

This site offers fishing and boating access to School Section Lake. Picnic tables are provided. Snowmobilers can ride to a public-funded trail just outside the site.

Directions: From Oconomowoc, take Highway 67 south through Dousman to County D. Travel west on County D to School Section Lake Road. Continue west on School Section Lake Road one mile to the access on the left.

Facilities: Picnic tables, outhouses.

Wanaki Golf Course

This golf course has a clubhouse with concessions, lockers, meeting rooms, a Pro Shop and indoor and outdoor dining.

Directions: From Menomonee Falls, take Highway 74 southwest to Lannon. In Lannon, take County Y (Lannon Road) south three miles to its junction with County K (Lisbon Road).

Facilities: Toilets, golf.

WAUPACA COUNTY

Contact: Waupaca County Parks and
Recreation Department
Courthouse
811 Harding St.
Waupaca, WI 54981
(715) 258-6243

Big Falls Pond Access

Featuring a shoreline with wooded areas and granite outcroppings, the access provides picnic tables, grills and a dock. Boaters and anglers can access Big Falls Pond and the north branch of Little Wolf River.

Directions: From Marion, take Highway 110 south to County C. Turn west and continue to Big Falls.

Facilities: Picnic tables, boat landing.

Chief Waupaca Park

A ¼-acre site dedicated to Chief Waupaca, the park includes a historical marker, grill and picnic area.

Directions: From Marion, take Highway 110 south 2½ miles. The park is on the east side of Highway 110.

Facilities: Picnic tables.

Gills Landing

A boardwalk in this 11.5-acre park, also referred to as Decker Memorial Park, stretches into a wetland marsh, where visitors can look out from an observation platform. The aquatic area features a seawall and provides fishing on the Wolf and Waupaca rivers. A picnic area and boat launch are also available.

Directions: Take Highway 110 south into Weyauwega. Turn east on County F (Alfred Street) and travel four miles to the park.

Facilities: Picnic tables, picnic shelters, outhouses, boat landing.

Graham Lake Access

Located north of Iola, this site provides access to Graham Lake, which feeds into the beginning of the south branch of Little Wolf River.

Directions: From Iola, take County J north to North Lake Road. Turn west and go one mile to Graham Lake Road. Turn south and go ½ mile.

Facilities: Boat access (no formal landing).

Grass Lake Access

Only a couple of miles from Graham Lake, this site provides access to Grass Lake.

Directions: From Iola, take County J north 4½ miles.

Facilities: Boat access (no formal landing).

Indian Crossing Park

Adjacent to Oakwood Park, this ¼-acre site marks the place where Native Americans crossed onto the chain of lakes. It includes a picnic shelter, bench swing and grills.

Directions: From the junction of Highway 49 and Highway 54 just west of Waupaca, travel a short distance on Highway 54 to County QQ. Turn south on County QQ and continue through King to County Q. Turn west on County Q and travel to the park, just northeast of the County Q bridge.
Facilities: Picnic tables, picnic shelter.

Keller Park

The granite outcroppings and scenic Pigeon River in this 19-acre park create the perfect setting for a picnic. Hiking trails follow the river's shoreline, which also provides opportunities for fishing and swimming. The park contains basketball and volleyball courts and a boat landing.
Directions: From Marion, travel south on Highway 110 to County G. Turn west on County G and travel 3½ miles.
Facilities: Picnic tables, picnic shelter, outhouses, swimming, beach, dressing rooms, hiking, volleyball, playground.

Kinney Lake Access

This site, just ½ mile east of Keller Park, offers a paved boat access onto the southeast side of Kinney Lake.
Directions: From Marion, take Highway 110 south to County G. Turn west and travel three miles to Kinney Lake Road. Turn north and continue to the access.
Facilities: Boat landing only.

Lembke-Long Lake Access

Located just east of Kinney Lake and Keller Park, this site provides direct access to Lembke Lake and access by channel to Long Lake. A picnic table is available.
Directions: From Marion, take Highway 110 south to County G. Turn west and go two miles to County S. Turn south and go 1½ miles to Long Lake Road. Turn east and go ¾ mile to the dead end.
Facilities: Picnic table, boat access (no formal landing).

Little Wolf Canoe Access

This access point is located seven miles upstream from Big Falls Pond on the north branch of Little Wolf River.
Directions: From Marion, take Highway 110 south to County C. Turn west and travel through Big Falls. Continue four miles west of Big Falls to Wolf River Road. Turn north and go 1½ miles to Norrin Road. Turn east and go ¼ mile.
Facilities: Canoe access (no formal landing).

Little Wolf Park

A small two-acre park, the site provides boat access on the southern shore of Manawa Mill Pond, thus also providing access to Little Wolf River. The park has an open shelter, grills and picnic tables, along with playground equipment.

Directions: From Manawa, take County N north ½ mile.

Facilities: Picnic tables, picnic shelter, outhouses, playground, boat landing.

Little Wolf River Boater Access

This one-acre site offers limited access for small boats onto the Little Wolf River. Picnic tables and grills are provided.

Directions: From Manawa, travel south on Highway 22/110. The access is on the west side of the road.

Facilities: Picnic tables, boat access (no formal landing).

Lowney-Rohan Wetland Preserve

During the spring and fall migrations, this 75-acre preserve attracts a large number of waterfowl and wetland bird species. Currently, bird watchers are limited to the parking lot, but an observation deck and informational displays are under development.

Directions: From Clintonville, take Highway 22/45 south to the junction with Highway 76. When Highway 45 continues south, veer off to the west on Highway 22. Continue one mile west on Highway 22.

Facilities: None.

Nelson Park

A pleasant site for fishing and picnicking on the Crystal River, the park features a footbridge to a small island and shoreline benches. There are also picnic tables and grills.

Directions: From Waupaca, take Highway 22 south 1½ miles to County K. Continue south on K 1½ miles.

Facilities: Picnic tables, outhouses.

North Branch Pigeon River Canoe Access

This five-acre site offers canoe access to the north branch of the Pigeon River and has picnic tables, grills and drinking water.

Directions: From Marion, take Highway 45 south one mile.

Facilities: Picnic tables, outhouses, canoe access (no formal landing).

North Lake Access

This five-acre site, situated between Graham and Grass lakes, features a "wet" trail and a small dock onto North Lake. Although walkers will get their feet wet on the trail, the connected deck boards allow visitors to enter a habitat they normally could not reach.

Directions: From Iola, take County J north four miles.

Facilities: Hiking, nature trail, boat landing.

Northland Park

Developed around the trout waters of Flume Creek, this park consists of a picnic area with tables, benches and a grill.

Directions: From Iola, take Highway 49 north eight miles.

Facilities: Picnic tables.

Oakwood Park

This 26.6-acre site in the Chain O'Lakes area features a nature trail with a railroad tie walkway leading to a small wilderness bog pond. The park also includes picnic tables, grills, a playground and a boat launch.

Directions: From the junction of Highway 49 and Highway 54 just west of Waupaca, travel a short distance on Highway 54 to County QQ. Turn south on County QQ and continue through King to County Q. Turn west on County Q and travel one mile to the park, which is adjacent to Indian Crossing Park.

Facilities: Picnic tables, toilets, hiking, nature trails, playground, boat landing.

Pigeon River Recreational Area

The north and south branches of the Pigeon River converge at this 40-acre site, which offers two picnic shelters. Trails and a footbridge are under development.

Directions: From Clintonville, take Highway 45 north to Knitt Road. Turn east and travel ½ mile.

Facilities: Picnic tables, picnic shelters.

Rollofson Lake Access

This site features a trail and wooden boardwalk extending into Rollofson Lake. A bench and floating dock are also provided.

Directions: From Waupaca, take Highway 49 north to Scandinavia. In Scandinavia, travel west on County B to County G. Turn north on County G and travel two miles to Bestul Road. Turn west on Bestul Road and travel three miles to Rollofson Lake Road. Turn north and go ½ mile.

Facilities: Hiking, nature trail.

Royalton Park

A two-acre park in the town of Royalton, Royalton Park contains a flower garden, picnic tables, grills and a swing set just west of the Little Wolf River bridge.

Directions: From New London, take Highway 45 north to Highway 54. Turn west on Highway 54 and travel to Royalton. The park is on the west side of Highway 54 in Royalton.
Facilities: Picnic tables.

Waupaca County Fairgrounds

Used primarily as a picnic site when not used for events, the fairgrounds offers a small playground, picnic tables and picnic shelters. For special occasions, visitors can rent the grounds and buildings, which include a racetrack, several livestock and exhibition buildings, and a covered grandstand outdoor arena.

Directions: Located in Weyauwega. Take Highway 110 into Weyauwega, then turn east on County F (Alfred Street). Continue to the junction of Alfred Street and Elizabeth Street.
Facilities: Picnic tables, picnic shelters, toilets, playground.

Waupaca County Forest

The 240 acres of county forest offer three miles of hiking, horseback riding, skiing and snowmobile trails. An arboretum and educational center are under development.

Directions: From Weyauwega, take Highway 10 south to County U. Turn south on County U and continue to Desert Road. Turn east and travel ¼ mile.
Facilities: Hiking, cross-country skiing.

White Lake Access

This ½-acre site offers access to White Lake, which features a small island, with a boat landing and small dock.

Directions: From Weyauwega, take Highway 110 north to Park Road. Turn north and go to the park.
Facilities: Boat landing only.

WAUSHARA COUNTY

Contact: Waushara County Parks Department
P.O. Box 300
Wautoma, WI 54982
(414) 787-7037

Big Hills Park

Located on Big Hills Lake, Big Hills Park is a popular spot for fishing. Anglers can catch pan fish and northern pike from the shore, or launch a boat and hook them on the water. The park also has picnic tables and a playground.

Directions: From Wautoma, take Highway 152 northeast to Mt. Morris. Turn east on County W and travel ¾ mile to County WW. Turn north and continue two miles to the park.

Facilities: Picnic tables, outhouses, swimming, playground, boat landing.

Curtis Lake Park

A pretty one-acre spot, Curtis Lake is a popular swimming and picnicking area. The park also has a playground and a boat launch.

Directions: From the junction of Highway 51 and Highway 21 in Coloma, take Highway 21 east six miles to Richford. Turn south on County B and travel ½ mile to County JJ. Turn east and go one mile to 10th Court. Turn south and continue one mile to the park entrance on the right.

Facilities: Picnic tables, outhouses, swimming, playground, boat landing.

Flynn's Quarry Park

Remnants of old quarrying structures still stand in this 48-acre natural area. The site has a number of hiking trails.

Directions: From Wautoma, take Highway 21 east to Lohrville. Turn south on County EE and travel ¾ mile to County N. Turn west and go ¾ mile to the park.

Facilities: Outhouses, hiking.

Hiking trails at Polk County's Lotus Lake Park beckon in fall when colorful leaves dot the paths.

Lake Alpine Park

Lake Alpine is a sand-bottom, manmade lake popular with families. The lake provides swimming and good fishing for children. Picnic facilities, a playground and a boat landing are also available.

Directions: From Wautoma, take Highway 21 east five miles to 22nd Avenue. Turn north and go ¼ mile to the park.

Facilities: Picnic tables, picnic shelter, outhouses, swimming, playground, boat landing.

Lake Huron Park

This small site offers fishing, swimming and boating on Lake Huron. The park also provides picnic tables.

Directions: From the junction of Highway 51 and Highway 73, take Highway 73 east to its junction with County P just past Plainfield. Continue east on County P three miles to 10th Drive. Turn south and travel 1½ miles to the park.

Facilities: Picnic tables, outhouses, boat landing.

Little Hills Park

While providing boating and fishing access to Hills Lake, this park also offers a quiet spot to picnic.

Directions: From Wautoma, take Highway 21 east two miles to 21st Court. Turn south and continue to Hills Lake.

Facilities: Picnic tables, outhouses, boat landing.

Kusel Lake Park

In winter, Kusel Lake Park features two intermediate cross-country ski trails totaling 8.8 kilometers. In summer, the park is popular for its swimming beach and large picnic areas. It contains two picnic shelters, a one-mile hiking trail, tennis courts, a playground and a boat launch. Anglers can try their lines in Kusel Lake.

Directions: From Wautoma, take Highway 22 north to Wild Rose. Turn east on County A and continue 4½ miles to 24th Avenue. Turn south and go one mile to the park.

Facilities: Picnic tables, picnic shelter, outhouses, swimming, beach, hiking, nature trails, cross-country skiing, tennis, playground, boat landing.

Marl Lake Park

Swimming is the major attraction at this 24-acre park. The park also has a picnic area with a shelter, tables and a playground. A boat launch allows anglers and boaters to enjoy the lake.

Directions: From Wautoma, take Highway 73 west ⅛ mile to County C. Continue west on County C six miles to 12th Avenue. Turn north and go ⅛ mile to the park.

Facilities: Picnic tables, picnic shelter, outhouses, swimming, beach, playground, boat landing.

Mt. Morris Hills Park

Mt. Morris Hills Park is the largest and most popular park in the county. The 300-acre site is also the county's highest point, offering a great view of the surroundings. It contains a picnic shelter, picnic tables, softball, tennis, horseshoes and a playground.

Directions: From Wautoma, take Highway 152 northeast to Mt. Morris. Turn west on County G and go ¼ mile.

Facilities: Picnic tables, picnic shelter, outhouses, toilets, baseball, tennis, playground.

Otto Brey Park

A six-acre site on Mill Pond, Otto Brey Park is a place for picnics and recreation. The park provides a picnic shelter, picnic tables, a softball diamond and a playground. Water enthusiasts can also enjoy fishing and boating on the pond.

Directions: From Wautoma, take Highway 21 east past Redgranite to Highway 49. Turn north and continue one mile to the park, near Auroraville.

Facilities: Picnic shelter, outhouses, baseball, playground, boat landing.

Pony Creek Park

A 16-acre park accessing Lake Poygan, this facility offers handicapped-accessible fishing and a walking trail along the shoreline. A launch is provided for canoeists, and picnic facilities are available.

Directions: From the junction of Highway 49 and County H in Poy Sippi, take County H east five miles to the park.

Facilities: Picnic tables, outhouses, hiking, nature trail, canoe landing.

Waushara County Fairgrounds

When it's not used for other purposes, the fairgrounds serves as a picnic site, with a shelter and tables.

Directions: In Wautoma, take Highway 21 (Main Street) to Fair Street. Turn south and go two blocks to the fairgrounds.

Facilities: Picnic tables, picnic shelter.

Waushara County Shooting Range

Located just outside Wautoma, this shooting range has unmanned 50-, 100- and 200-yard targets during the spring, summer and fall.

Directions: From Wautoma, travel west ⅛ mile on Highway 73 to County C. Continue west three miles to the shooting range.
Facilities: None.

Willow Creek Park

A quiet one-acre park, Willow Creek Park is known for its trout stream. Picnic tables are provided. In the winter, the park has a 2.4-kilometer beginner's cross-country ski trail.

Directions: From Wautoma, take Highway 152 northeast to Mt. Morris. Turn east on County W and go ½ mile.
Facilities: Picnic tables, outhouses, cross-country skiing.

WINNEBAGO COUNTY

Contact: Winnebago County Parks Department
500 East County Road Y
Oshkosh, WI 54901
(414) 424-0042

Asylum Point Park

This 56-acre park, dedicated to wildlife habitat restoration, offers excellent shore fishing, although many anglers venture into the lake to catch walleye, smallmouth bass and white bass. Situated on the shore of Lake Winnebago, the terrain ranges from lakefront to marshland to prairie. An additional 17 acres, currently being leased from the DNR, provides a boat launch and an island picnic area.

Directions: From Oshkosh, take County A north to Snell Road. Turn east and go ½ mile to Sherman Road. Turn south and continue to the park.
Facilities: Outhouses, toilets, boat landing.

Black Wolf Boat Landing/Nagy Park

This park provides access to Lake Winnebago and includes picnic facilities, a harbor and a boat launch. During the summer months, anglers frequent the park to hook perch and walleye in the nearby mud flats and reefs.

Directions: From Oshkosh, travel south on Highway 45 for eight miles.
Facilities: Picnic tables, toilets, boat landing.

Boom Bay Boat Landing

This landing derives its name from the rafts of logs or "booms" that logging companies once secured in a section of the bay north of the current launch area. The current landing opens onto the east side of Lake Poygan.

Directions: From Neenah, take Highway 150 west past Winchester to County M. Turn south and go ½ mile to County MM. Turn west and continue to Richter Lane. Turn north and continue to the landing.
Facilities: Outhouses, boat landing.

Eureka Boat Landing

A huge fishing site, this landing is especially popular in the spring, during the walleye and bass runs on the Fox River. Anglers also pursue catfish from a wharf along the shoreline or from boats, which can be launched from three ramps at the landing. Picnic tables and a shelter are provided.

Directions: From Omro, take Highway 21 west to County K. Turn south and continue to Eureka. The landing is off County K in Eureka on the Fox River.
Facilities: Picnic tables, picnic shelter, outhouses, boat landing.

Grundman Boat Landing and Park

Anglers and boaters can access Lake Winnebago from this park, which offers three launch ramps and two docks. The landing provides access to some of the better walleye and perch spots on the lake. The shoreline also creates a scenic picnic spot.

Directions: From Oshkosh, take County A north 3½ miles past Winnebago. Turn east on Grundman Lane to the landing.
Facilities: Picnic tables, outhouses, toilets, swimming, boat landing.

Lake Butte Des Morts Boat Landing

Popular for its fishing and boating access onto Lake Butte Des Morts, this landing provides a handicapped-accessible fishing pier, harbor and boat launch. Anglers can try their luck at snagging a walleye or a muskellunge. Visitors also enjoy the picnic facilities, which include a shelter, tables and a playground.

Directions: From Oshkosh, take Highway 21 west to Sandpit Road. Turn north and go one mile to Leonard Point Road. Turn west and go ½ mile to the landing.
Facilities: Picnic tables, picnic shelter, outhouses, playground, boat landing.

Lake Poygan Boat Landing

This landing provides access to the south shore of Lake Poygan, which offers excellent fishing year-round. The site also provides picnic tables.

Directions: From Winneconne, take County B west eight miles.
Facilities: Picnic tables, outhouses, boat landing.

Lake Winneconne Park

A 28-acre site, this park is one of the most heavily used in the county. It offers access to Lake Winneconne from a beach and a boat landing and has an island-protected channel for overnight mooring. Visitors also appreciate the picnic shelter, picnic tables, playground and areas for playing baseball, volleyball and horseshoes.

Directions: Located in Winneconne, the park can be reached by taking Highway 116 to 3rd Avenue. Turn north on 3rd Avenue and continue to the park.

Facilities: Picnic tables, picnic shelter, outhouses, toilets, swimming, beach, dressing rooms, baseball, volleyball, playground, boat landing.

Lasley Point Archaeological Site

Located on the site of an old Oneota Indian village, the area now serves as an archaeological and natural site. Although most of the relics have been removed to museums, visitors can explore the natural beauty of the second-growth forest through a number of hiking trails on the 47-acre site.

Directions: From Winneconne, take Highway 116 east to County M. Turn north and go one mile to Lasley Point Road. Turn west and go ½ mile.

Facilities: Hiking.

Sunnyview Exposition Center and Fairgrounds

Primarily used for a wide variety of events such as festivals and meetings, this 78-acre countryside site serves picnickers and campers at other times. Adjacent to Winnebago County Community Park, the grounds contain 120 trailer and tent sites. Picnic tables are also provided.

Directions: From Oshkosh, take Highway 45 north to County Y. Turn east and go ½ mile.

Facilities: Picnic tables, toilets, tent sites, trailer sites.

Waukau Creek Nature Preserve

This preserve features Waukau Creek, formally known as Rush Creek. Densely wooded ravines slope into the floodplain, providing a naturally beautiful setting for a picnic or a hike.

Directions: From Omro, take Highway 116 south to Waukau. Go north on Dehli Road ¼ mile past County K.

Facilities: Picnic tables, outhouses, hiking, nature trails.

Winnebago County Community Park

A complete recreational facility adjacent to the county fairgrounds, this park features two fishing lakes and a swimming beach. It also offers picnic areas, a one-mile exercise course, three ball diamonds, a 12-field soccer complex, an archery range, a BMX track, tennis courts and a playground.

Directions: From Oshkosh, take Highway 45 north to County Y. Turn east and go ½ mile.
Facilities: Picnic tables, picnic shelters, toilets, swimming, beach, nature trail, baseball, tennis, playground.

WOOD COUNTY

Contact: Wood County Parks Department
Courthouse
400 Market St.
P.O. Box 8095
Wisconsin Rapids, WI 54495
(715) 421-8480

Dexter Park

A 1,200-acre site, this large park contains a scenic hiking trail along the Yellow River that serves as a cross-country ski trail in the winter. Although much of the park has been left wild and undeveloped, other areas are well-developed, with a swimming beach, picnic areas and facilities for baseball, volleyball and tennis. The park also has a playground, boat landing and 96 campsites.
   Directions: From the junction of Highway 13/73 and Highway 80 just north of Pittsville, take Highway 80 south six miles from Pittsville to the junction with Highway 54.
   Facilities: Picnic tables, picnic shelter, toilets, tent sites, trailer sites, swimming, beach, dressing rooms, hiking, nature trail, cross-country skiing, baseball, volleyball, tennis, playground, boat landing.

Nepco Lake Park

The only access point to 494-acre Nepco Lake, the park is used primarily for water recreation, such as waterskiing, boating, fishing and swimming. Nepco Lake County Park also has hiking and cross-country ski trails, handicapped-accessible paths, a playground, picnic tables and grills.
   Directions: Just south of Wisconsin Rapids on Highway 13, turn east on Griffith Avenue (County Z).
   Facilities: Picnic tables, toilets, swimming, beach, dressing rooms, hiking, nature trails, cross-country skiing, playground, boat landing.

North Wood Park

North Wood County Park features a 225-foot suspension bridge over the Yellow River. It provides access to two small fishing lakes and a swimming beach. Picnic tables and shelter, 100 campsites, a playground and facilities for baseball and volleyball are also available.

> **Directions:** From the junction of Highway 13/73 and Highway 80 at Pittsville, take County A north five miles.

> **Facilities:** Picnic tables, picnic shelter, outhouses, toilets, tent sites, trailer sites, swimming, beach, dressing rooms, baseball, volleyball, playground.

Powers Bluff Park

The highest point in the county at 1,472 feet, Powers Bluff Park has historic Indian dance rings and burial grounds. Seventy of the park's 160 acres are designated as a Scientific Preservation Area. The rock outcroppings in the park create the setting for a scenic picnic or a hike on a 1.5-mile self-guided nature trail. In the winter, a shelter offers fireplaces for visitors needing to warm up after cross-country skiing, downhill skiing and tubing. Grills and a playground are also available.

> **Directions:** From Marshfield, take Highway 13 south to Highway 10. Turn east and continue to County E. Turn south and continue to the park, just past the junction with County N.

> **Facilities:** Picnic tables, toilets, hiking, nature trails, cross-country skiing, playground.

Richfield 360 Acres

These 360 acres of gently rolling, undeveloped land offer eight miles of wooded hiking or cross-country ski trails. The site is divided by Puff Creek, a small creek which runs into Yellow River. Campers can also hike into seven wilderness campsites if they first obtain a permit.

> **Directions:** From the junction of Highway 13/73 and Highway 80 at Pittsville, take County A north seven miles.

> **Facilities:** Toilets, tent sites, hiking, nature trails, cross-country skiing.

Seneca ATV Area

This day-use 400-acre area provides 12 miles of developed ATV trails on county forest land. A picnic shelter and picnic tables are available.

> **Directions:** From Wisconsin Rapids, take Highway 54/73 south to Port Edwards. Continue west on Highway 54 and travel three miles.

> **Facilities:** Picnic tables, picnic shelter, toilets.

South Wood Park

At this park, a four-mile multi-use trail stretches around Lake Wazeecha for hiking, biking and other recreation. Seventy-three campsites are available, 40 with electricity. Water activities such as waterskiing, fishing and swimming are also popular. The park contains two beaches, picnic areas, two community buildings, a baseball diamond and a boat landing.

Directions: From Wisconsin Rapids, take County W east 5¼ miles to County U. Turn south to the park.

Facilities: Picnic tables, picnic shelter, outhouses, toilets, tent sites, trailer sites, swimming, beaches, dressing rooms, hiking, baseball, playground, boat landing.

Squaw Creek Pond Area

Known primarily for its fishing, this five-acre area features the bass-stocked, four-acre Squaw Creek Pond.

Directions: From Marshfield, take County Y east one mile to Stadt Road. Turn north and travel ½ mile to Trout Drive. Turn west and go ¼ mile to Squaw Creek Pond.

Facilities: None.

Index

More Books on Wisconsin

FROM WISCONSIN TRAILS

Great Weekend Adventures
from the Editors of *Wisconsin Trails*

Best Wisconsin Bike Trips
by Phil Van Valkenberg

Best Canoe Trips of Southern Wisconsin
by Michael E. Duncanson

Great Golf in Wisconsin
by John Hughes and Jeff Mayers

Wisconsin, The Story of the Badger State
by Norman K. Risjord

Barns of Wisconsin
by Jerry Apps

Mills of Wisconsin
by Jerry Apps and Allen Strang

WISCONSIN TRAILS
P.O. Box 5650
Madison, WI 53705
(800) 236-8088